Checklists
for Life

Checklists for Life

104 Lists to Help
You Get Organized,
Save Time, and
Unclutter Your Life

Kirsten M. Lagatree

RANDOM HOUSE
NEW YORK

This book is for
Leo Takuma Lagatree

And in memory of his great grandparents
Leo Daniel McCormick
and
Katherine Darmody McCormick

Contents

Acknowledgements

There are many people whose generous assistance helped make this book possible. Special thanks to my friend, Catherine Carlisle. Her advice and editorial assistance on matters as diverse as children, the law, personal organization, and the importance of having a really good time as often as possible can be found throughout this book.

I'd also like to express my love and gratitude to my multi-talented family for their significant contributions: My brother Bruce Lagatree, for his consistently wise and patient help on questions relating to computers and home repair; my sister Marion Lagatree, for her prompt and generous response whenever I had a question on crime prevention or personal safety; and my brother Donald Lagatree, for sharing his hard-won experience and secrets for growing gorgeous flowers and vegetables while foiling insects and other pests.

Thanks to my good friend Cai Glushak, M.D., FACEP, Emergency Medical Services Director at The University of Chicago Hospitals, for his great wit and practical advice on first aid and general medical questions and to Susan Fuchs, M.D., Associate Professor of Pediatrics, Northwestern University Medical School for answering questions on children's health and first aid. Edward Fleegler, M.D., FACEP, an internist in Bryn Mawr, Pennsylvania, was an excellent resource on medical checkups for men and women over age 40.

Thanks and hoison sauce to food writer Candy Sagon of the *Washington Post* for her practical and imaginative advice on stocking a kitchen pantry. Stuart Feil, writer, editor, computer meister, and generous friend, provided invaluable guidance on buying computers and keeping them healthy.

Appreciation to Jennifer Cockburn for her help with foreign phrases and to John E. Barth, Geoff Baum, Deb Cohen, Tad Daley, Lucia de Lisa, John Dimsdale, Kitty Felde, Sandy and Bob Hobbs, Kathy Merritt, Annie, Frank, and Suzanne Paine, Sharon Weissman (and many others I'm sure I'll think of when it's too late to add their names), who contributed enthusiasm, ideas and information. I'm especially grateful to my professional accomplices: my savvy agent Nancy Yost, who came to me with the idea for this book and then helped make it happen; and my dear friend and talented editor Page Edmunds, who made working on the book a joyful experience. As always, love and thanks to my husband John Barth, who served gourmet dinners every night and made the cats run on time while I was absorbed in list-making.

I happily acknowledge the help I've received from so many people, but must insist any mistakes that may have wormed their way between these pages be credited to me alone.

Introduction

The world is made up of two kinds of people: Those who write lists to make sure they take care of everything that needs to be done, and those who prefer to wing it. Winging it does add a certain excitement to life—it's been known to involve such adventures as getting by without clean underwear during lengthy vacations. But as the appeal of such adventure wears thin, many wing-it folks become converts to list-making.

In fact, there's something about the human psyche that actually craves lists. Some people find them so deeply reassuring that they just can't stop making them. As a list-maker myself, I offer you a few of the reasons why—in list form, of course:

- Lists make us feel free, not because they help us remember things, but because they allow us to forget them. When the important stuff is written down, the mind is free to wander, to create, or to think deeply about life's complex questions. (Iced cappuccino or double latte? Mountain cabin or Caribbean villa?)
- Lists help us face life with confidence. No challenge is so formidable that it can't be wrestled into list form and mastered, one checkmark at a time.
- Few gratifications in life can match the one that comes from marking a big, bold ✔ through each task as it's dispatched. (Many dedicated list-makers will admit to including completed tasks on our lists, just for the satisfaction of checking them off!)

Show me a consistently successful person and I'll show you a list-maker. Individual styles may vary: some people jot lists neatly on notepads, some scribble them hastily on anything they can find, still others depend on lists they find in books! Whatever the form or source of the list, the important thing is that successful people depend on them. Lists ensure that the job gets done correctly and completely—*and* with the added finesse that springs from an uncluttered mind.

In case you're worried, reading this book will not turn you into a nervous or compulsive person. To the contrary: you'll feel well prepared for anything life tosses your way and you'll learn to relax in a manner you never dreamed possible. Even those extended vacations will seem more enjoyable—after all, there's nothing like the quiet confidence that comes from knowing you've got a suitcase full of clean underwear.

Kirsten M. Lagatree

Personal Safety

Most of staying out of harm's way comes down to using common sense: Lock your house and car, know who to call when you need help, and be prepared for emergencies. Easier said than done! We often postpone doing what we know we should, or let common-sense safety precautions slide entirely, in the haste and distractions of daily life. These lists will tell you what you need to do and what you should have on hand to prevent—or deal with—emergencies, so you can be calm and efficient when it really matters.

How to Avoid Being a Victim

Next to common sense, your best personal safety tool just might be your "uncommon sense," your intuition. Take yourself seriously if you sense danger or have a bad feeling about a person or situation. Do not be embarrassed or afraid to offend: Get away immediately. The National Crime Prevention Council suggests these ways to keep yourself safe wherever you are.

AT HOME

1. **Don't hide house keys in planters,** mailboxes, under doormats, or in other common (and obvious) places.

2. **Don't put your name or address on your keys.** Losing them irretrievably is much better than giving a criminal the key to your house and car.

3. **Don't open the front door without finding out who it is.** Verify the identification of service personnel, even if you are expecting them.

4. **Don't rely on door chains.** They can easily be kicked in or otherwise broken.

5. **Never give personal information** to unknown or "wrong number" callers. This includes your phone number, social security number, credit card number, and address.

6. **Don't reply to harassing phone calls.** Hang up immediately.

IN PUBLIC

1. **Stay alert to your surroundings.** Take note of who is behind and ahead of you. Use your peripheral vision to keep track of anyone gaining on you.

2. **Get away.** Don't second-guess your instincts just to avoid embarrassment or give someone the benefit of the doubt. If you think you're being followed, cross the street if possible and go to a well-lit place where there are other people.

3. **Carry a shrill whistle** and don't be embarrassed to use it if you suspect you may be in danger.

4. **Always walk as if you know exactly where you are going.** Stand up straight and make brief,

self-confident eye contact with people around you. Police believe that rapists and muggers target victims who appear vulnerable, weak, easily intimidated, or who seem to be daydreaming. Conduct yourself accordingly!

5. **Hold on to your valuables.** Women should carry their purses close to the body. Men should carry wallets in inside coat pockets, not pants pockets.

6. **Don't look like an easy target.** Avoid carrying large amounts of money and wearing obviously expensive jewelry. Handle your money and credit cards carefully; try not to display them while making transactions.

7. **Plan the safest route when walking**—day or night. Avoid alleys, vacant lots, deserted streets, and construction sites.

8. **Lighten your load.** Avoid walking with a large load of packages or grocery bags. They slow you down and make it difficult to react quickly.

9. **On public transportation:**
   • Avoid sitting near doors and exits. You are more vulnerable to being robbed or attacked by a criminal on foot.
   • Be aware of who gets off a bus or train with you. If you think you're being followed, walk directly to an area with other people and good lighting.

10. **In an elevator:**
   • Take a quick look before getting in an elevator. If someone suspicious is on board, or gets on with you, back out and wait for another car.
   • Stand near the elevator controls.
   • If you are attacked, hit the alarm and as many floor buttons as possible.

IN THE CAR

1. **Lock your door** and keep the windows rolled up. Always lock the doors when you park your car, no matter where you are or how brief a time you'll be away.

2. **Look around.** Check the front and back seats and floors of your car before getting in.

3. **Keep your car well maintained** and the gas tank at least half full. This will lessen the chance of your being vulnerable on the highway.

4. **If your car does break down,** put up the hood and lock your doors and windows. Set out flares if you have them and use your cell phone to call for assistance. If a stranger stops to help and you don't have a phone with you, roll the window down an inch or so and ask him to call police or a tow truck. (See page 277, "What to Carry in Your Car").

5. **Don't drive home** if you're being followed. Go to a police station or a well-lit service station where you can use the phone. Never get out of your car unless you're positive you can get inside safely.

6. **Don't pull over** if someone tries to force you off the road. Get a description of the vehicle and write down the license number. Drive immediately to a police station or any open business and report the incident to the police.

7. **Don't stop** if a passing motorist indicates something is wrong with your vehicle. Drive to a well-lit area with people around before stopping to check your car.

8. **Don't stop in an isolated area** to help someone who appears to have a disabled vehicle. Drive to a phone and call for help instead.

9. **Don't stop for flashing headlights** or another signal from another car unless you see the blue or red lights of a police vehicle.

10. **Put your purse on the floor** of the car while you're driving. Leaving it conspicuously on the passenger seat could tempt a thief to break in and grab it.

11. **Never pick up hitchhikers.** Need it be said?

If You Are Attacked

1. **Staying calm is your best defense** because you'll be better able to judge the situation and consider your options.

2. **If the attacker is unarmed**—and if you sense you could get away—fight back. But not getting injured is your first priority. If the attacker has a weapon, don't take the risk of resisting.

3. **If your life is threatened,** do anything you can to hurt your attacker and get away. Concentrate your attack at the eyes and groin. If you're holding your keys, jam them right into the eyes if you can. Don't wait to check the effect, run away as fast as you can.

4. **You may be able to avert an attack** by behaving bizarrely. Experts suggest acting crazy, picking your nose, throwing up—whatever comes into your head.

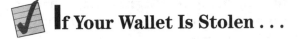

If Your Wallet Is Stolen . . .

When your wallet is stolen, you have two major issues to deal with. They are (to paraphrase the old Jack Benny joke) your money and your life. A thief with your driver's license and credit cards can use the contents of your wallet to obtain a new set of identification documents in your name—making your funds and your credit line completely accessible. Following the steps in this checklist will help ensure that your identity as well as your money and credit are protected.

1. **Report the crime** to the police right away and get a copy of the police report. You may be asked for it later by your credit card companies, your insurance company, your bank, or other agencies to verify the crime.

2. **Call each credit card company** to report the theft right away. If you're away from home, ask a family member, neighbor, or house sitter to pull your master list of credit card numbers and other relevant information from your files to make sure you cancel every card. (See page 29, "Records and Documents You Need at Home.")

3. **Report the theft to the three major credit reporting agencies,** Experian (formerly TRW), 800-682-7654; Trans Union, 800-916-8800; Equifax, 800-685-1111. This alerts them to halt any credit checks that could be the result of a thief shopping in your name.

4. **If your checkbook or ATM card was taken,** call your bank immediately and stop payment on outstanding checks that don't sound familiar. Request new bank accounts, a new ATM card, and a new PIN.

5. **If you have a safe deposit box at the bank,** call that department to report the theft.

6. **Notify the passport office** to watch for anyone using your identification to obtain a fraudulent passport.

7. **Inform your local and long distance telephone carriers** and your utility companies that someone might try to open service in your name.

8. **If your keys have also been stolen,** change all the locks on your home and car.

9. **After the theft:**
   - Monitor your credit card and bank statements carefully for charges that occurred after the theft and that might have slipped past officials at these agencies.
   - Order your credit report from all three agencies (Experian, Trans Union, Equifax) at least quarterly, to catch possible fraudulent use of your credit.

Important Numbers to Keep by Your Phone

Look up the numbers below before you need them (most emergency numbers are on the first page of your local phone book) and keep them near your home telephone. To make sure emergency numbers are easy to find when you need them, laminate a list and attach it to the refrigerator, or tape it inside a cabinet door near the phone. Include important information that anyone calling from your home would need to report in an emergency, such as your street address and phone number.

EMERGENCY PHONE NUMBERS

1. **911.** This number should only be used when you need immediate assistance from the police, the fire department, or an ambulance. If you're tempted to use it for less serious reasons, imagine getting a 911 busy signal if you or a family member needed immediate help. Teach your children how to dial 911 and make sure they know how to give their home address.

2. **Police emergency.** Most cities have a number to call other than 911 for situations that are urgent, but non-life-threatening, such as traffic accidents.

3. **Police nonemergency.** This number is for occasions when you want to report stolen or vandalized property or any matter that requires a police report, but doesn't require immediate response.

4. **Work telephone and cell phone.** Even if your children have these numbers memorized, it's a good idea to have them posted in case they forget, or if anyone else needs to reach you in an emergency.

5. **Fire department.** In case of fire, call 911. When neither life nor property is immediately threatened—if you smell something burning, but can't confirm a fire—use the nonemergency number.

6. **Poison control center.**

7. **Doctor and pediatrician.**

8. **Dentist.**

9. **Veterinarian.**

10. **Emergency vet information.** The University of Illinois at Champagne-Urbana offers twenty-four-hour poison control help for animals for a $30 fee at 800-548-2423. Ask your own veterinarian what other emergency numbers you should have on hand, including the nearest twenty-four-hour emergency clinic for off-hour emergencies. (Make sure you know where the clinic is, and how to get there.)

 ## FREQUENTLY CALLED NUMBERS

1. **Electrician.**

2. **Plumber.**

3. **Neighbor.** List at least one who would be available to come over if needed. You may know your neighbor's number by heart, but post it next to the phone for anyone else who might need assistance while in your home.

4. **Newspaper circulation department,** to report missed papers or to suspend delivery during vacations.

5. **Pharmacy.** Your pharmacist is a good person to call for questions about side effects and interactions of over-the-counter and prescription drugs.

6. **Children's schools,** for reporting absence, tardiness, and so forth. Also keep numbers for coaches, tutors, and music instructors where you can find them.

7. **Hair salon and barber.**

8. **Auto mechanic.**

9. **Auto insurance agent.** Put your policy number right next to the phone number.

10. **Housekeeper.**

11. **Home maintenance.** Keep numbers for any services you regularly receive, such as gardeners or pool cleaners.

12. **Restaurants,** including take-out places for delivery, and favorite eat-in restaurants for making quick reservations.

13. **Movie theaters.**

14. **Baby-sitters.**

15. **Pet sitters and dog walkers.**

16. **Florist.**

17. **Train information.**

18. **Bus information.**

19. **Taxi services.**

20. **Airlines.** List your frequent flyer numbers next to the airline's phone number.

21. **Bank.** Keep your account numbers next to the phone numbers.

✓ Everyday Burglar-Proofing for Your Home

There's no foolproof way to foil a clever or determined burglar. But there are several things you can do to protect your home from a crook who's looking for an easy mark. According to the National Crime Prevention Council, half of all burglaries occur because residents have neglected to lock doors and windows—proof that minimal security can make a big difference. Take these easy steps to secure your home.

1. **Lock doors and windows** before leaving the house. Make it a habit to check them at night.

2. **Get pick-proof locks** for all your windows.

3. **Install dead bolts** on your front and back doors. Anything else can be more easily broken.

4. **Put a dowel or broom handle** in the track of sliding-glass doors so they can't be opened even if the lock is tampered with.

5. **If there's a pane of glass within easy reach** of an inside door lock, consider getting a lock that only opens from inside with a key.

6. **Plant prickly or very thick shrubs and plants** under your windows to create a physical barrier.

7. **Install motion detector lights outside,** especially in back or side yards where burglars like to hide.

8. **If you've been thinking of installing window bars** or a home alarm system, don't put it off. If you don't have a security alarm system it can't hurt to place stickers in your windows indicating that you do. As always, the idea is to deter a burglar looking for an easy mark.

9. **Keep expensive equipment** and other valuables away from windows where they can easily be spotted from outside.

10. **Join or start a neighborhood watch group.** Neighbor-to-neighbor networks are one of the most effective ways to discourage crime.

✓ Securing Your Home While You're Away

In addition to the burglar-proofing tips above, take the following precautions whenever you're going to be away for an extended time. You can discourage intruders by creating the impression that someone is in the house or will return shortly.

1. **Keep drapes and shades** as you normally have them. Don't make the mistake of giving your house that "closed for the season" look with every window shuttered.

2. **Hire a house sitter** or have a neighbor come in to turn on lights and open and close drapes.

3. **Stop your newspaper delivery** and have your mail held at the post office. Piles of papers are a sure sign that no one is home.

4. **Set a few timers** and set them to turn lights on and off at different times in different parts of the house, echoing your typical patterns.

5. **Leave a car parked** out front or in the driveway. Or invite a neighbor to park there every day or so. If you live in a snowy area, arrange for someone to shovel your walk and driveway, or even just to drive in and out of your driveway when it snows to create the impression that someone is home.

6. **Adjust your answering machine message** if necessary. You may want to tell callers that you'll "be back shortly" so scammers don't hear an invitation to an empty house.

7. **Put away large trash cans,** outdoor furniture, or anything else that could provide climbing assistance to intruders.

8. **Consider buying a safe.** If you don't have a safe, you may want to hide small items like jewelry or cash in unlikely places (see below for suggestions).

9. **Leave the radio or TV on.** It can't hurt.

Best and Worst Places to Hide Valuables

Since you can't guarantee an intruder won't get into your home, it's important to think strategically about hiding valuable items inside. Indoors, your best defense is a good offense: make the burglar's job as difficult as possible.

 ## THE WORST PLACES TO HIDE VALUABLES

1. **Jewelry boxes.** If you use a traditional jewelry box, hide it. Consider storing jewels in less obvious containers (see below).

2. **Dresser tops and accessible drawers.** Don't keep cash or jewelry on dressers, in sock or underwear drawers, or in any drawer that's in easy reach and can be rummaged through quickly.

3. **Under the mattress or beside the bed.** Many burglars look in these places first, especially when they're checking for weapons.

 ## THE BEST PLACES TO HIDE VALUABLES

1. **Your closet** may be a good spot to tuck your jewelry box.

2. **A sewing kit** or tackle box can harbor cash or items of jewelry without offering temptation to a burglar.

3. **Clever decoys** are among the best places to hide and disguise your valuables. False wall outlets don't provide electricity, but they do provide a good hiding place (you can plug cords into these or put furniture in front to make them more realistic and less

obvious). Fake food or cleaning product cans and hollow books are also widely available.

4. **The bathroom** is bypassed by most burglars, unless they're looking for prescription drugs. Avoid the medicine cabinet, but stash items in other bathroom cupboards, especially among cleaning supplies.

5. **Kitchens** offer hiding places where burglars may not look. Consider wrapping jewelry or cash in foil and storing it in the freezer.

6. **Basements** are good places for valuables because burglars don't want to take the time and trouble required to rummage through them.

Tip Many cities have stores known as "Cop Shops" which sell burglar-foiling devices. Call your local police department for information on your nearest store.

☑ Common Home Accidents and How to Avoid Them

No matter what kind of work you do, or how good it feels to come home after a rough day at the office, safety statistics suggest you'd be better off staying at work. More people in this country die from accidents at home than at work—five times as many! More people are disabled in home accidents than in work injuries and car crashes *combined*. National Safety Council president Jerry Scannell stresses that all home accidents are preventable. Here are the most common home accidents and the NSC's recommendations for preventing them.

1. **Falls.**
   - Fasten carpet edges securely and put nonslip mats under area rugs.
   - Keep telephone and electrical cords where they can't be tripped over.
   - Put away toys, clean up clutter, and move obstacles out of walkways.
   - Wipe up all spills immediately.
   - Use nonskid tub and shower mats and install grab bars in toilet and bath areas.
   - Equip all indoor and outdoor staircases with securely fastened handrails along both sides. When it snows, use salt or cat litter on sidewalks and driveways to prevent slipping.

2. **Poisoning.** More than one million children under age five are accidentally poisoned every year.
   - Lock drugs, household cleaners, and other potentially hazardous substances where children can't get to them.
   - Don't leave children unattended in a garage,

bathroom, kitchen, or any place where potential poisons are kept.

- Never store household cleaners in unmarked containers where they might be mistaken for something safe to drink.

3. Fire. Smoke detectors reduce the chance of fire fatalities by 40 to 50 percent, according to the National Fire Protection Association.

- Install a smoke detector in each bedroom and at least one on every floor of your home.
- Make sure your family is well drilled in an escape plan, including two ways to exit every room. Practice regularly so everyone learns to respond automatically and without panic.

4. Electrical shocks. Ground-fault circuit interrupters (GFCI) are electrical outlets with quick-tripping circuit breakers that instantly shut off power if an appliance plugged into them overheats or comes in contact with water. They are now required in all new construction and remodeling jobs in bathrooms, kitchens, laundries—wherever shock hazards are greatest. If your home doesn't have these life-saving electrical outlets, consider having them installed by an electrician.

BE PREPARED FOR EMERGENCIES If an accident does occur, or if a family member becomes ill suddenly, knowing what to do immediately can make the difference between life and death. Have each member of the family take age-appropriate first aid and CPR classes. Post a list of emergency numbers next to the telephone (see page 8). Put together a survival kit in case of disasters (see page 26). Remember that seconds count in a fire.

Top Twenty Safety Items for Your Home

Here are the top twenty home-safety items recommended by the National Safety Council. Every item you have on hand decreases the risk that someone in your home will die or be injured in a preventable accident.

1. **Smoke detectors.** Change the batteries twice a year when you change your clocks. The National Fire Protection Agency (NFPA) recommends that you replace your smoke detectors after ten years and test them once a month to be sure they work.

2. **Carbon monoxide detectors.** The NFPA recommends these alarms for households with attached garages and those with fuel-burning appliances or fireplaces.

3. **Ground-fault circuit interrupters.** These electrical outlets with quick-tripping circuit breakers help prevent death or injury from electrocution and can be installed by an electrician. (See page 18 for more detail on how they work.)

4. **Fire extinguishers.** A multipurpose dry chemical class ABC type is the best fire extinguisher for home use. Keep one in the kitchen, one in the bedroom, one near the fireplace, and one in your car. Make sure everyone in the household knows how to use them. Check the extinguishers periodically and replace them when they expire.

5. **Emergency evacuation plan.** Come up with a plan for escaping in a fire and for natural disasters. Make sure everyone in the house participates in the practices.

6. **Flashlights.** Keep a flashlight under or near each person's bed and one in the basement. If you live in

an area with frequent power failures, buy a few of
the kind with a large base so they don't have to be
hand held if the power is off for several hours.
Check batteries every few months and store a supply of extra batteries where you can find them easily.

7. **First aid kit.** See page 24.

8. **List of emergency phone numbers.** See page 8.

9. **Shutoff valve tags.** Label the turnoff valves for
gas, oil, and water and clearly mark the main electricity shutoff. Know how to use each in case of
emergency.

10. **Grab bars.** Since falls are among the leading
causes of home accidents, and bathtubs are among
the slipperiest surfaces, anchor grab bars into the
wall studs in tubs and showers.

11. **Slip-resistant finishes.** Use nonslip mats or
strips or decals in bathtubs and showers to help prevent slipping.

12. **Safety glazing.** Every glass pane in your house
should be shatterproof. Look for a mark in the lower
corner showing the manufacturer's name and type
and thickness of safety glass. Don't forget shower
and patio doors.

13. **Handrails.** Indoors or outdoors, every staircase in
your home should have secure handrails on both
sides.

14. **Step stool/utility ladder.** Keeping a lightweight,
sturdy step stool in an convenient spot will decrease
the likelihood of anyone taking chances standing
on a chair or other dangerous perch.

15. **Sufficient lighting.** Help prevent falls with
nightlights near bedrooms and bathrooms. Keep interior and exterior stairways and walkways adequately lit.

16. **Tested appliances.** Every electric and gas appliance in your home should carry the Underwriters Laboratories (UL), Canadian Standards Association (CSA), or American Gas Association (AGA) designation.

17. **Safety goggles.** These are an absolute necessity when using certain tools; they're also recommended by the NSC for indoor cleaning and garage and yard work.

18. **Survival kit.** See page 26 for details on what to include.

19. **Childproofing.** See page 155 for information on how to childproof your home.

20. **Pool safety.** Homes with swimming pools should have the following:
    - A four-foot fence with self-closing and latching gate
    - Life preservers
    - Rescue equipment
    - Lockable cabinet for storing pool chemicals
    - Poolside telephone

What to Keep in Your Medicine Cabinet

When you're stocking your medicine cabinet, think about common illnesses and discomforts. First shop for those and then add any other over-the-counter medications required by members of your family. If you stock up on the items on this checklist, you'll be prepared to cope with a wide range of minor maladies. It's also a good idea to check with your doctor and your pharmacist for other medicine cabinet suggestions.

1. **A fever reducer and pain reliever such as Tylenol** or other aspirin substitutes containing acetaminophen. Many medical experts recommend taking nonaspirin remedies for fever and pain because they're less likely to irritate or upset the stomach.
2. **Ibuprofen.** An anti-inflammatory used to reduce pain and swelling. It should be given only to adults because its use has not been proved safe in young children. Advil and Motrin are common brands.
3. **Aspirin.** It is wise to keep aspirin on hand in case someone in the house has a heart attack. Aspirin is a blood thinner and chewing one while dialing 911 could save a life. Aspirin should never be given to children or teenagers because its use by young people has been associated with Reye's syndrome, a rare but sometimes fatal condition.
4. **Antibiotic ointment** for cuts, scrapes, or burns.
5. **Hydrocortisone cream** for rashes and other skin irritations.
6. **Hydrogen peroxide** for cleaning wounds and disinfecting minor cuts.

7. **Antihistamine** (for colds, allergies, itching). Benadryl is the most commonly known name in antihistamines.

8. **Decongestants and cough remedies** (suppressants and expectorants) for cold symptoms.

9. **Soothing lozenges** for sore throats.

10. **Antacids.**

11. **Antidiarrhea medication.**

12. **Band-Aids.**

13. **Tweezers.** (Keep matches nearby to disinfect before using on splinters, ticks, etc.)

14. **Thermometer.**

15. **Cotton balls** and swabs for applying medication.

✓ What to Keep in a First Aid Kit

Every family should have at least two well-stocked first aid kits. Keep one in your car and one at home, in a spot where you can get to it easily but small children cannot. (And don't forget to take the first aid kit when your family goes away on vacation.) Check your kits every few months and replace any missing items or expired medications. Buying a preassembled first aid kit can be a convenient starting point, if you add any items that are on this checklist but not in the kit. Items that overlap with the contents of your medicine cabinet need only be kept in your car kit.

1. **First-aid manual.**

2. **Sterile gauze pads** (4×4 and 2×2 size) and rolls of gauze for wrapping.

3. **Adhesive tape.**

4. **Adhesive bandages in various sizes.**

5. **Scissors.**

6. **Elastic bandage** (Ace, for example).

7. **Safety pins** for making slings (you can use a towel, diaper, or other cloth for an emergency sling).

8. **Latex or thin plastic medical gloves.**

9. **Peroxide for cleansing wounds and dissolving blood stains.**

10. **Antiseptic liquid or ointment** (Betadine, polysporin, etc.) and antiseptic wipes (these might be best for an automobile kit).

11. **Small plastic bags** to make ice packs (keep ice on hand in the freezer; or a bag of frozen vegetables will work as an ice pack in a pinch.)

12. **Benzocaine spray** for minor burns and abrasions.

13. **Hydrocortisone cream** for minor inflammatory skin conditions (get a doctor's diagnosis if condition lasts more than twenty-four to forty-eight hours).

14. **Benadryl** or other antihistamine tablet to relieve itching.

15. **Ibuprofen.** Many doctors now prefer it to aspirin or Tylenol for fever and recommend ibuprofen for children under twelve, who should avoid aspirin.

16. **Saline eye drops.** Keep a large bottle to flush chemicals or foreign matter from eyes.

17. **Tweezers.** (Keep rubbing alcohol or matches nearby to disinfect them before use.)

18. **Thermometer.**

19. **Mouthpiece for administering CPR.** These can be purchased from your local Red Cross chapter. They range in price (and sophistication of design) from $2 to $12. They are sometimes given free to those who take rescue breathing (CPR) classes.

20. **Cotton swabs** for applying ointment or cleaning small areas.

Tip If you plan to keep syrup of ipecac on hand to induce vomiting in cases of accidental poisoning, talk to your doctor, who can advise you when *not* to use it. In certain situations, such as loss of consciousness or ingestion of caustic substances, it can be dangerous. Never administer ipecac until you've called your poison control center and discussed the situation with an expert.

✔ What to Keep in a Disaster Kit

The secret to coping as calmly as possible with an emergency is to be ready before it happens. Earthquakes, hurricanes, blizzards, and other natural disasters are unnerving enough. When they cut off access to power, water, groceries, and other necessities, they can be both frightening and disorienting. But if you've stockpiled essentials ahead of time and coached your family on disaster preparedness, you will have as much protection as you can.

A 30-gallon trash can, a large plastic storage bin, or any other durable, reasonably light container with a tight-fitting lid will make a fine disaster kit. Store the kit in a garage, basement, or any out-of-the-way place that is large enough to accommodate it and reasonably easy to get to. (You won't want to climb into the attic in some types of emergencies.)

1. **Tools.** Pipe and crescent wrenches, screwdriver, crowbar, and any tools required to turn off utilities if necessary. Ask your utility companies how to turn off gas, water, and electricity in an emergency. Don't turn off the gas unless you're certain there is a leak. You may have to wait days to have it restarted by the gas company.

2. **Heavy protective gloves.**

3. **Candles and matches.** Keep them in a watertight container within the kit.

4. **Battery-operated radio.**

5. **Flashlight.**

6. **Extra batteries for radio and flashlight.**

7. **Fire extinguisher.**

8. **"Swiss Army" knife.**

9. **Can opener.**

10. **Eating utensils.**

11. **Disposable plates** (paper, Styrofoam, or plastic).

12. **Aluminum foil.**

13. **Plastic trash bags.**

14. **Extra blankets.** You can buy emergency foil blankets (which store very compactly) at camping or sporting goods stores.

15. **First-aid kit** (see page 24).

16. **Personal items.** Pack toothbrushes, toothpaste, razor, combs, soap, and other items your family will want for personal hygiene.

17. **Warm clothes and sturdy shoes.** The shoes can be especially important if floors are covered with broken glass. A heavy sweater for each family member will come in handy if your home is without heat. If you live in an earthquake zone, keep your sturdy shoes under the bed in case a quake hits at night. If you need to be prepared for a severe weather disaster or an evacuation, store the shoes and warm clothes near the top of the kit where they'll be easy to get to.

18. **Money.** Hide enough cash to get your family by for at least three days. See page 15 for "Best and Worst Places to Hide Valuables."

19. **Nonperishable food.** Store enough prepared food that doesn't need heating to feed your family for at least three days. It's a good idea to choose foods your family enjoys (and to include candy bars and other treats) to keep morale and energy up. To keep your emergency stash fresh, rotate the food (including canned goods) into your pantry at least every year and substitute with newly purchased items.

20. **Bottled drinking water.** One gallon per person, per day for at least three days is the rule of thumb. Store water in airtight containers and keep the jugs away from gasoline or other products with poisonous fumes. Replace the stored water twice a year (changing the water when you turn your clocks for daylight savings will help you remember to do it) and use the old water to drench the garden.

21. **Bleach or disinfectant tablets.** If water has been contaminated with bacteria, you can purify it by adding a teaspoon of bleach per gallon of water or disinfectant tablets according to the manufacturer's directions.

BE PREPARED
- To prepare for a possible evacuation, put important family documents together in a small plastic container and know the location of the mementos and heirlooms you would grab if authorities ordered you to leave immediately.
- Keep your vehicle's gas tank at least half full at all times and fill it up at the first mention of possible severe weather.
- To prepare for any disaster, designate an out-of-state relative or friend to be called in case the household gets separated. That way, each person will know the others are accounted for, even if they can't get in touch with them right away.

Getting Organized

2

Let's face it, life is easier, less frustrating, and, well, involves a lot less swearing when you can find what you're looking for right when you need it. As my grandma (maybe yours, too) used to say, "A place for everything, and everything in its place." Maybe that's why she lived so long and swore so little.

Records and Documents You Need at Home

The items on this checklist should be kept where they are easy for you—or anyone in your family—to locate without too much detective work. (See page 33, "Nine Steps to Organize Your File Cabinet.")

1. **Will** (original or a copy depending on your lawyer's advice) and estate planning documents.

2. **Cemetery deeds and burial instructions** (copies).

3. **Safe deposit box contents.** Keep a list of the contents of your safe deposit box as well as copies of the original documents kept there on file: birth and death certificates, deeds to property, vehicle owner-

ship titles, military records, citizenship papers, adoption, custody, divorce decrees, etc.

4. **Insurance policies.**

5. **Household inventory** (see page 250).

6. **Copies of receipts for major purchases** (clip originals to the home inventory list stored in your safe deposit box).

7. **Appliance and equipment instructions and warranties** with serial and model numbers.

8. **Credit card information.** Keep a list of all cards, account numbers, PIN numbers, and phone numbers to call if the cards are lost or stolen.

9. **Medical/health records** for each member of the family.

10. **Education records, diplomas, and transcripts.** You may wish to keep originals in your safe deposit box.

11. **Passports.** If you prefer, store them in your safe deposit box, and keep only passport numbers at home.

12. **Bank statements.** Just to be safe, keep them for seven years.

13. **Credit card statements.**

14. **Investment records.**

15. **Tax records.** The IRS has a three-year statute of limitations on auditing returns. But they can go back as far as six years if auditors suspect fraud. Check with your accountant to be sure you're following the most up-to-date regulations on saving returns.

16. **Employment records.**

✅ **W**hat to Keep in Your Safe Deposit Box

Here is the acid test for what you should store in your safe deposit box according to the Federal Deposit Insurance Corporation (FDIC): Would you be in deep trouble without this item? If the answer is yes, it goes in the box.

Staying out of "deep trouble" by storing your valuables at a bank is relatively affordable. Depending on the size of the safe deposit box, and on your bank, a year's rental will cost from $25 to $90.

Put original documents in the box and keep photocopies at home so you'll be able to get to them quickly if necessary.

1. **Estate planning documents:** wills, trusts, powers of attorney. Talk to an attorney about whether the *original* or a copy of these documents should be kept in your safe deposit box. The answer will depend on what your state law says about who (if anyone) will have immediate access to your safe deposit box after your death.

2. **Deed to your house** and any other property, including burial plot at cemetery.

3. **Vehicle titles.**

4. **Birth, marriage, death certificates;** military records, adoption, custody, divorce, legal change of name, and citizenship papers.

5. **Complete home inventory,** including appraisals, receipts, and photographs or videos of all your insured items. (See page 250 for tips on creating a home inventory.)

6. **Stock certificates,** savings bonds, and other securities.

7. **Diplomas and transcripts.**

8. **Extremely precious jewelry,** coins, stamps, or other valuable collections.

Tip You can make sure your safe deposit box is not sealed and made inaccessible by the state or a probate court after your death by renting it jointly with a spouse, adult child, or other trusted person. Anyone whose name is on the rental contract will have uninterrupted access to the box.

✓ Nine Steps to Organize Your File Cabinet

Almost everybody hates to do filing. It's not the sheer boredom of the task that makes it so awful, it's the agony of facing all those pieces of paper that require your Solomon-like wisdom: Keep this or throw it away? If I keep it, where should I file it? If I file it, how will I know how to find it again?

Creating a well-organized place for your files will make the job more bearable, and may help establish a regular filing session before paperwork builds up to an overwhelming pile.

1. **Purchase a filing cabinet.** Tucking bills, receipts, insurance policies, and other vital paperwork into a drawer here and a shoebox there leads from disorganization to chaos. Bite the bullet and buy a good-quality suspension file cabinet that allows drawers to be pulled out to their full length. This way you can see and reach every folder comfortably—no small thing when you're trying to work quickly and efficiently.

2. **File alphabetically.** The two most commonly used filing systems are organization by category (Financial, Legal, Personal, etc.) and organization by alphabetical listing. Professional organizer Barbara Hemphill, author of *Taming the Paper Tiger,* makes a very good case for the alphabetical system: "There are always gray areas when you begin categorizing. In filing everything strictly by the alphabet, there is no question of where to look." File related documents under the letter of the "umbrella" subject— "T" for Travel, for example—so you'll never have to wonder where to look for what you need. Here are a few examples of this method:

- File under "C" for Car: Maintenance records, owner's manual, warranties, copies of registration documents.
- File under "I" for Insurance: Auto, home, health, life, and other policies, each with a separate folder naming the type of policy. (You won't look for your car insurance policy in the "Car" file because you know *all* your policies are in the "Insurance" file.)
- File under "S" for Safe Deposit Box: A list of the box's contents. You can also use this file as a storage area for documents you plan to take to the box the next time you go to the bank. You might even keep the key in this file.
- File under "R" for Restaurant: Any restaurant reviews you want to keep, plus a list of friends' recommendations and restaurant phone numbers. This is just an illustration, of course. If restaurants aren't your passion, maybe you'd create a file under "S" for software reviews, or under "G" for information on golf courses around the world, or articles about gardening. In any case, name the file according to the specific topic. A folder called "Hobbies" or "Special Interests" will quickly become crowded and disorganized.

3. **Create subfiles.** Making separate files for categories within categories (Insurance, Auto; Taxes, 1999; Travel, Australia) will keep your file folders from becoming fat and unwieldy. It will also make it easier to keep the information within each folder organized and easy to get to.

4. **Block out an afternoon.** Setting aside three or four hours will keep you from giving in to distractions and abandoning the job before you've made significant progress. It's also good for morale when you know there's an end in sight. If you aren't able to finish the job in the first session (and few people

will be), set another date with your files in the near
future.

5. **Give yourself elbow room.** Whether you're
   starting from scratch or reorganizing an existing filing cabinet, do the sorting on a floor or large table-
   top where you can spread out without crowding.

6. **Sort.** This is the part most people dread. But when
   you've already determined that every item will be
   filed according to its individual name, deciding
   which paper goes where will be a less burdensome
   chore. Print the name of each file and its subcate-
   gories on separate index cards and tape them down
   to help you quickly spot the stack where each document belongs.

7. **Weed.** You will be amazed at the amount of Juras-
   sic paperwork you unearth: instructions and warranties for products you no longer own; expired
   grocery coupons, brochures for products that no
   longer interest you; business cards from . . . who
   was that guy?; multiple catalogs from the same
   company. Toss what you don't need.

8. **Label.** This is a no-brainer. Simply write a file
   folder label corresponding to those index cards you
   used for sorting (by this time you will have worked
   most of the kinks out of the system and decided exactly what you'll call each file). Use your best print-
   ing and a sharp pen, so your labels will be easy to
   read and won't smear or rub off.

9. **File!** Transfer your piles of paper into the labeled
   folders and put them into the drawers in alphabetical order.

Tip Use hanging file folders with plastic stand-up tabs rather
than manila folders, which can slide down in the drawer
and easily become dog-eared. If your filing cabinet
doesn't have metal frames for hanging folders, they are
easy to find at most office supply stores.

Nine Steps to Organize Your Workspace

The axiom that work expands to fill the time available can be applied equally well to storage: papers, files, and miscellaneous clutter expand to fill all available space. A messy desk and chaotic filing system waste time and siphon productivity—and sanity. Once you've worked your way through this checklist, you'll have a workspace that makes you look forward to getting down to business every day, whether in your study at home or at the office.

1. **Take a deep breath.** If you're starting out with an intimidating pile of "stuff" on and around your desk, don't despair. Take a deep breath and devote a small amount of time—half an hour—daily to sifting through it. If you do a little organizing each day, you *will* reach the bottom of the stack!

2. **Ask questions.** As you go through your stacks of paper, piles of files, mountains of magazines, etc., ask yourself: Do I need this? Why? What happens to it next? Where will I look for it when I want it? Don't ask "where should I put it?" Your organizing system is only as good as your ability to remember where you put things!

3. **Categorize paperwork.** Organizing guru Barbara Hemphill advises separating the papers you keep into either "action" (you must do something about it) or "reference" (you'll be consulting it for information from time to time).

4. **Use two trash cans.** If you keep papers because you aren't sure whether or not you'll need them again, institute a two-step trash system. Use a small container for papers and other items that are clearly trash. Use a large wastebasket for anything you're

not entirely sure about tossing. Empty it only every few weeks so you can rescue papers you later decide you need.

5. **Clear your desktop.** Reserve the surface of your desk for items you use daily. Your in-out box, Rolodex, computer, diskette file, calendar, message pad, and anything else that's part of your daily routine belong there. Supplies you only reach for occasionally (stapler, extra pens, writing paper, file labels, etc.) should be stored in your desk drawer where they will be easy to reach, but not in the way.

6. **Purge desk drawers.** Remove anything from your desk that you use less than once a week and put these items, along with spare supplies, in a cabinet, credenza, or storage closet.

7. **Put files away.** Try to keep only one project at a time on your desk. When you finish with a file, put it away, even if you'll need it later. This habit clears your workspace and your mind for the task ahead.

8. **Shelve reference material.** Put a shelf over your desk for reference books and manuals you reach for frequently. This way they're always at hand, but never in the way.

9. **Conduct regular cleansing rituals.** The only way to maintain the organization you worked so hard to achieve is to turn your "sort and trash" exercise into a weekly ritual. Set aside time to do this regularly so you'll never have to confront an overwhelming mess again.

Say Cheese! How to Organize Your Photographs

Many of us "sort" our photographs by dumping them into shoeboxes or shopping bags anticipating the lazy, rainy afternoon we'll spend leisurely catching up on our photo albums. The fact is, it would take a rain of biblical proportions—forty days and forty nights—to make the time for this project and the longer you await the perfect day, the more jumbled those boxes and bags become. Stop waiting: get those photos organized now and then go out and take some more—rain or shine!

1. **Weed ruthlessly.** Wouldn't it be nice if all your pictures turned out perfectly every time? You save yourself a lot of storage space by pretending they did, and getting rid of pictures you don't like. If Uncle Charlie's elbow covered the baby's face, toss the picture! If the photo is nearly perfect, except that it's overexposed, throw it away! If you hate that picture snapped while you were chewing steak, out it goes!

2. **Don't save duplicates.** If you order duplicates so you can send photos to grandparents, or to pass along to friends who are in the shot, by all means, share them. Then throw the rest away.

3. **Make your negatives positive.** Throw away negatives except those for photos you may want to duplicate. Place them in a plain white envelope and write the date and a brief description on the outside. Attach the envelope to the inside of the album where the pictures are displayed or file it in the back of the appropriate photo storage box.

4. **Decide how to sort.**
   - Chronological order—This is the way most photo albums are organized. But if you've kept pictures

in shopping bags or shoeboxes for any length of time, reconstructing a full chronology could scare you off forever.

- By occasion—Christmases, birthday celebrations, etc.
- By year—This is a broad category, but it begins to impose some order.
- By trip—Regardless of the system you use for the rest of your photos, you may find it rewarding to put major trips (for example, "France 1995," "Costa Rica 1982") in special albums.

5. **Album alternatives.** Not every photo worth saving must be placed in an album. Consider purchasing photo filing boxes, which are less demanding of your arranging skills and deliver faster results. They're sturdier and more attractive than shoeboxes and have tabbed dividers and plastic photo protection sleeves inside. Their most winning feature is that they don't ask much of you and will enable you to find a particular photo whenever you're looking for it.

✔ **N**ine Steps to Organize Your Clothes Closet

Raise your hand if you open your closet each morning and serenely retrieve the very garment you had in mind. (Martha Stewart, put your hand down.) For the rest of us, this doesn't have to be a fantasy. An organized, user-friendly closet is well within reach—and your clothing will be too, when you're finished with this checklist. All you'll need to make this dream come true are a few uninterrupted hours and a supply of gritty determination. It may help to invite a friend in as referee.

1. **Shovel it out.** Unless you're lucky enough to own a cavernous walk-in closet, you need all the space you can get. Find another place for your tennis racquet, the ugly lamp, the rolls of wrapping paper, and anything else you were storing in your closet until you could figure out what to do with it. If you can't find homes, or uses, for these articles, put them in a box to donate to charity.

2. **Be ruthless.** Toss or donate anything you haven't worn in two years. Wedding dresses are excepted. Salmon pink dyed-to-match bridesmaid shoes are not.

3. **Be brave.** Try on the clothing you intend to keep. This is a tedious and occasionally depressing chore. But if you don't like what you see in the mirror when you're wearing those pants, why keep looking at them hanging in your closet? Ask a good friend to help you judge.

4. **Arrange by category.** Group like items, hanging shirts with shirts, slacks and pants all together, and so on. If you have room, store your out-of-season clothes and rarely worn items like formal wear sepa-

rately. If not, put them in the least accessible part of the closet.

5. **Sort by color.** Now arrange the groups of similar items by color, from lightest to darkest shades. When one glance at your closet tells you what clothes go well together, you'll dress with far more speed and style. You'll also become aware of colors you've overstocked, those you may need to buy more of, and any colors that stand out like a sore thumb (usually a fashion error warning sign).

6. **Save steps.** Store your socks right in the closet so you can see them as you select the slacks and shoes you'll wear. Several rolled pairs fit nicely in a shoe-box and the boxes can be stacked to accommodate an infinite number of socks (or stockings). Make selection quick and easy by labeling them ("Browns," "Blacks," "Blues," etc.) or purchase acrylic boxes you can see through.

7. **Be nice to your sweaters.** Store your sweaters gently in the folded position and they'll repay you by looking splendid year after year. Suspend them cruelly from hangers and they'll take revenge by developing funny-looking shoulders and drooping to outlandish lengths. If you have space, keep the folded sweaters in clear acrylic stacking boxes on the floor or on shelves in your closet. Protect them by tossing in moth-repellent herbal sachets.

8. **Discipline your shoes.** A shoe rack or two will transform that unruly mob of footwear on your closet floor into ranks of neatly paired shoes.

9. **Accessorize decisively.** Purchase an assortment of those inexpensive and convenient hangers designed especially for ties, belts, or scarves. When your ties are near your shirts, belts next to pants, and scarves right next to blouses, you'll be perfectly coordinated before you even have your first cup of coffee.

Stocking Up

It's the little things in life that matter—especially when you don't have them when you need them. The catch is that the only way to have what you need *when* you need it is to buy what you need *before* you need it. How do you deal with that dilemma? These lists will help you anticipate those little things in life you're going to need.

Kitchen Equipment: What to Have on Hand

If you haven't cooked much, or at all, or haven't been near the kitchen for a very long time, there's no reason you can't start now. Take this checklist to the kitchen-ware section of your favorite store and you'll come home with the basic tools to stock your kitchen and whip up a few simple and delicious meals.

 BACHELOR'S BASICS

1. **Knives.** One small (4–6-inch) paring knife; one 8–12-inch all-purpose knife (sometimes called a chef's knife); one 13–16-inch serrated (saw-tooth) knife for slicing bread. Don't waste your time or

money buying cheap knives. They are much harder—and more dangerous—to use because they aren't always sturdy enough for the job (the blade can snap off), and they dull very easily, which increases the risk of slicing something you weren't aiming at (like your finger). By the time you replace a few cheap knives, you might as well have enjoyed the use of a good one to begin with. If you only buy one, make it a large paring knife.

2. **Vegetable peeler.** Even if you buy your carrots bagged and precleaned and like to mash your potatoes with the skins on, you'll need a vegetable peeler sooner or later for *something*. If you are left-handed, buy one designed for lefties.

3. **Cutting boards.** At least a small one for mincing garlic, cutting a single piece of fruit, or doing any small job; consider an additional, larger board for bigger jobs and slicing loaves of bread. Buy washable plastic (polyethylene) that you can clean at the sink or put in the dishwasher. Figure on replacing the boards (for health reasons) a couple of times a year, or whenever they've accumulated a number of slash marks.

4. **Saucepans.** A 1-quart pan for heating up a can of soup, making oatmeal for two, or boiling an egg; a 2–4-quart pan for steaming rice or vegetables, boiling potatoes, and so on.

5. **Kettle or Dutch oven.** Buy a heavy pot that distributes heat well (cast iron with enamel finish or heavy gauge anodized aluminum are two possible choices). Make sure it has a tight fitting lid (check it for wobble). You'll use this pot for everything from creating homemade soups to boiling pasta or cooking corn on the cob for a crowd.

6. **Skillets.** An 8-inch nonstick for frying up a couple of eggs and a second 12–14-inch pan for stir-frying and sautéing. When you're skillet shopping, look

for sturdy pans that will distribute heat well and resist warping. You're usually safe with heavy nonstick aluminum or enameled cast iron; but iron pans are heavy. Heft a few (with one arm) to make sure you'll be comfortable using them.

7. **Toaster or toaster oven.** A toaster oven is more versatile, but if all you want are some crispy slices to go with your morning coffee, a wide-slot toaster will do the job quickly and with less attention needed from the cook.

8. **Baking pans.** Look for metal pans or glass baking dishes. A 9×9 square and a 9×13 oblong will give you a good start on baking anything from cornbread to chicken to lasagna. You may want to consider the nonstick option if you go with metal. If you prefer glass, buy the oven-to-freezer-to-microwave type for maximum versatility. You can buy casserole dishes with covers, if you like; or you can just wrap foil tightly over the top of anything you're baking that needs to be covered (unless it's going in the microwave!).

9. **Mixing bowls.** You may find it convenient to own a nesting set of several bowls. But buy at least two so you'll be prepared for scrambling one egg or tossing salad for a group.

10. **Colander.** A must-have if you're going to be cooking pasta. Metal or plastic is fine; just remember that metal will be hot after you've poured boiling water through and plastic will melt if you put it near a stove burner.

11. **Grater.** You'll use this for preparing the cheese for your Mexican pizza or for shredding carrots for a salad.

12. **Cookie sheet.** If you like to bake large batches of cookies, having more than one cookie sheet will make the job go faster. If your baking is minimal,

you will still want at least one cookie sheet for baking pizzas or putting under things that may drip. Buy heavy-gauge, nonstick cookie sheets. They'll last longer, be easier to clean, and burn many fewer cookies than their flimsy counterparts.

13. **Can opener.** A hand-held opener with a comfortable grip will do nicely. But if you love gizmos or plan to eat an exclusively canned diet, go ahead and get an electric opener. If you do go electric, have a backup in case the power goes out and you need to make tuna sandwiches for dinner.

14. **Pepper mill.** There are times when nothing but freshly ground pepper will do. You don't need to buy an expensive or fancy one; just make sure it's convenient to fill.

15. **Dry and liquid measuring cups.** All measuring cups are not equal. Cups for dry ingredients usually come in 4-cup plastic sets (¼, ⅓, ½, 1 cup) which make it easy to level off the top with a knife for an exact measurement. Liquid measurers are most often glass, with a pouring spout and a little extra room to prevent spills. A Pyrex 2-cup measure is most convenient.

16. **Measuring spoons.** Get a set of metal spoons linked together; they are sturdy and can go in the dishwasher.

17. **Utensils.** Wooden spoons, soup ladle, pasta tongs, pancake turner, rubber spatula.

18. **Oven thermometer.** You would be amazed at the temperature variations in standard ovens. It's not uncommon for a household oven to be off by as much as 50 degrees or more. Use the thermometer to get a rough idea of how your oven's temperature corresponds to its dial setting. That way you can decide whether to have your oven recalibrated or just to compensate for the difference when you set the

dial. Keep a thermometer in the oven to continue monitoring its accuracy.

19. **Tea kettle.** Choose one that whistles and won't rust inside. You can always boil water in a saucepan, but it's tacky, takes longer, and wastes energy. Plus, you can leave a tea kettle sitting on the stove and it looks cozy.

20. **Plastic containers.** You'll be more likely to save those delicious leftovers if you can just toss the extra mashed potatoes into a plastic bowl with a matching lid. Putting the entire pot in the refrigerator only works until you run out of pots or room in the fridge. Buy a set of plastic bowls with snap-on lids at the grocery or kitchen supply store or wash and save margarine and take-out containers.

21. **Potholders.** Buy a couple of flat ones and an oven mitt or two. Don't try to use dishtowels: they don't provide adequate insulation and a pan's heat will quickly penetrate a damp towel, creating steam, which can give you an especially nasty burn.

Tip When you're buying cookware, it makes sense to spend the money for good quality. Cheaply made pots and pans wear out much faster than good ones. Even worse, they're more likely to warp, leaving you with pans that wobble on the stove. Cheap pans also burn food more easily because they don't conduct heat well. All around, inferior pots and pans make cooking considerably more difficult and frequently less successful.

NICE, BUT NOT ESSENTIAL

1. **Coffee grinder.**
2. **Coffee maker.**
3. **Large salad bowl.**

4. **Meat thermometer.** Using a meat thermometer is the only sure way to tell if your roast beef, pork, or turkey is properly cooked. An instant read thermometer is very convenient—and can also be used to check the doneness of burgers or other meats that you're cooking on the grill or stovetop.

5. **Potato masher.**

6. **Large slotted spoon.**

7. **Salad spinner.**

8. **Sharpening steel.** This is a long, straight piece of metal used to sharpen knives. You grasp the wooden handle and run the knife along the steel. It's worth the extra two minutes it takes to sharpen a knife before you use it—or at least right before you carve a roast, slice a tomato, or embark on any job that requires a good sharp edge.

9. **Wooden toaster tongs.**

10. **Whisk.** One large and one small in stainless steel would be ideal. It's great to grab a small one to whisk a couple of eggs together in a small bowl or measuring cup; and a large whisk will help you quickly blend a bowl of pancake or other batter. But if the idea of owning even one whisk makes you nervous, you *can* get buy on the smaller jobs with a fork.

11. **Garlic press.** This can be a good shortcut for chopping or mincing garlic.

12. **Hand-held electric mixer.**

13. **Blender.**

14. **Fine mesh strainer.**

15. **Vegetable steamer.**

Dinner from Thin Air: A Kitchen Pantry Checklist

With the right ingredients in your pantry, fridge, and freezer you can always have the makings of a quick, easy, and delicious dinner, even on a busy weeknight. Take this checklist to the grocery store and you'll be surprising family and friends with your ability to pull dinner from thin air.

 IN YOUR CABINET

1. **Extra-virgin olive oil.**

2. **Vegetable oil.**

3. **Balsamic and red wine vinegar.**

4. **Dijon mustard.**

5. **Fresh garlic.**

6. **Soy sauce.**

7. **Dried oregano, basil leaves, thyme, rosemary, cayenne pepper.** Keep in mind that there are literally dozens of herbs and spices out there—these are some of the most versatile.

8. **Cinnamon.** You'll be amazed what a great combo chicken and cinnamon make. (See "Weeknight No Brainers.") Plus, cinnamon toast is comfort food.

9. **Salt and pepper** (fresh ground and canned pepper).

10. **Canned beans.** Refried, garbanzo (also called chickpeas), black, or any favorites can be added to rice or pasta to make a complete protein and a satisfying as well as nourishing dish. Also add beans to tossed salads, tuna, or other main dish salads.

11. **Pasta.** Stock at least one long and one short pasta for variety. Remember, the thinner the pasta, the quicker it cooks.

12. **Couscous.** Check the gourmet or international area of your store for flavored couscous (garlic and olive oil, lentils and tomatoes, etc.). Many can be prepared in under ten minutes with virtually no effort and the result is a tasty one-dish meal.

13. **Rice.** Stocking different kinds, like basmati or long-grain white rice, along with a couple of pilaf mixes will give you more options for main and side dishes. Steer clear of Minute Rice. Real rice only takes about fourteen minutes longer, and when it's cooked, it tastes like rice—not the box it came in. Spend those extra fourteen minutes opening the mail or playing with your cat.

14. **Bottled pasta sauce.**

15. **Bottled salsa.**

16. **Canned tomatoes.** Chopped or crushed, in their own juice. Add to pasta or rice for a no-cook sauce, or use as a base for a more complicated red sauce.

17. **Raisins.** Add these to salads, fruit salads, couscous.

18. **Bottled marinated artichoke hearts, roasted red peppers, mushrooms.** Lay these out on a plate with some oil-packed tuna for a quick antipasto dinner. Or add any of these things to hot pasta with sauce or to any dish that seems to need a little jazzing up.

19. **Canned tuna and salmon.** Use for salads, pastas, and, yes, even sandwiches.

20. **Canned chicken or vegetable broth.** Stock a few 14 ½-ounce cans and use for soup base or instead of water for more flavorful rice. Using low-sodium broth will allow you more control over the flavor and salt content of what you're cooking.

21. **Boboli** or other commercially made pizza shells. Try the "no brainer" Mexican pizza on page 53 or let your kids construct a weeknight pizza of their own invention.

 In Your Refrigerator

1. **Eggs.** Never underestimate the simple elegance of an herb (cheese? vegetable? onion?) omelet for dinner.

2. **Butter or margarine.** (or both) butter can be kept frozen.

3. **Plain nonfat yogurt.** Mix a cup of yogurt with ¼ cup extra virgin olive oil, one large clove of garlic (pressed), salt and pepper. Use as sauce on chicken, fish, or rice. Sprinkle in thyme or dill if the mood strikes you.

4. **Parmesan cheese.** A tightly wrapped wedge will keep for weeks. Stay away from the dust-flavored "cheese" sold in round cans in the grocery section.

5. **Cheddar and/or jack cheeses.** They don't keep as long as parmesan (which is much drier), but wrap them tightly and cut off any visible mold before using. Toss cubes into salads, grate into Mexican dishes, or slice for snacks.

6. **Pecans and pine nuts.** Toast either in a small skillet and add to salads, pastas, rice dishes.

7. **Bagged whole baby carrots.** Sauté or steam them for a side dish, slice them for a salad, or just snack on them while you're cooking dinner.

8. **Onions.**

9. **Potatoes.** Bake a big one (sweet or russet) as the centerpiece of the meal and top with salsa, yogurt, grated cheese, black beans, diced onion, or any combination that appeals to you.

In Your Freezer

1. **Pesto sauce.** Thaw this in the microwave and add to pasta or use as a topping on pizza shells or lightly toasted French bread.

2. **Bread and rolls.** Crusty rolls, baguettes, sourdough bread—keep as much as you can fit in the freezer and heat gently in a 300-degree oven. Never use the microwave to thaw or heat frozen bread or you'll need a hacksaw to slice it.

3. **Sausages.** Better groceries sell fully cooked, frozen chicken sausages flavored with delicious additions such as apple, sun-dried tomatoes and parmesan or cilantro. You can defrost these and pop them into a skillet—they'll be ready as soon as they're heated through.

4. **Frozen vegetables.** Let your preference be your guide, of course, but here are some possibilities: Peas thawed quickly under cold running water are a tasty addition to salads and pasta. Frozen spinach sautéed with garlic, olive oil, and rosemary is an excellent side dish for pasta. In a pinch, you can stir-fry good-quality frozen green beans, broccoli florets, and snow peas with any other vegetables as a side or vegetarian main dish.

5. **Chicken breasts.** The skinless/boneless variety can be thawed in the microwave.

WEEKNIGHT NO-
BRAINERS
FIVE DINNERS SO
SIMPLE YOU HARDLY
NEED A RECIPE
Any of these quick and easy one-dish dinners can be good enough for company. Round out the meal with salad, bread, and dessert and serve the feast with speed *and* pride.

Mexican Pizza: Layer refried beans, salsa, and grated jack or cheddar cheese on pizza shells. Bake in moderate oven until heated through.

Speedy Salad: Add canned tuna or salmon to a bed of fresh greens, sliced sweet onion, carrots, blanched and chilled frozen green beans, toasted pine nuts (and anything else that sounds good to you). Toss the whole thing with bottled dressing or a vinaigrette.

Darmody Chicken: Put boneless chicken breasts in a shallow baking pan and sprinkle lightly with cinnamon; add several bagged baby carrots and sprinkle them with dill; next put in a few quartered potatoes and onions; place a few cloves of garlic, peeled and sliced, on and near potatoes and chicken. Sprinkle thyme, salt, and pepper over everything and drizzle with a small amount of olive oil. Bake uncovered at 350 degrees until chicken is done and potatoes, carrots, and onions are tender (about 40 minutes).

Pasta and Sauce: Toss cooked penne, angel hair, or any other favorite pasta with bottled pasta sauce that you've heated in the microwave. Add garbanzo beans to make a complete protein and add peas too if you like them. Grate fresh parmesan over top.

Couscous and Sausage: Use your favorite flavored couscous; before you boil the water, put in a dash of cayenne pepper and a couple tablespoons of raisins. Toast pine nuts or pecans while the couscous is steaming. Toss the cooked grains with garbanzo beans and nuts. Serve this with sautéed or microwaved chicken sausages.

Stocking a Linen Closet

Whether you view sheets and towels as essential elements of household décor or think of them in strictly utilitarian terms, stocking your linen closet with attractive, good-quality sheets and towels is both practical and satisfying. Here's what you should have on hand.

 ## BED LINENS

Considering that a third of our lifetime is spent in bed, sheets and pillowcases that feel good next to the skin also make a big difference on a daily basis. Industry expert Liz Hough of Cotton Incorporated says sheets with a higher thread count (the number of threads in a square inch of fabric) last longer, and "the more you wash them, the softer they become." If you have sensitive skin, or just enjoy the feel of soft sheets, you'll be happier with a minimum 200-thread count. Not surprisingly, the price of the sheet goes up with the thread count, but you don't have to spend a fortune to get good ones. Watch for sales, especially department store "white sales" in January and July.

1. **Sheets.** Two sets per bed will allow you to have one in the wash and one on the bed. A third (or even fourth) set is fun if you enjoy giving your bedroom a new look by changing the sheets. Make sure you have at least one set of sheets for every bed in the house, including sofa beds for those times when everyone comes to stay at once.

2. **Pillowcases.** Keep the same number of pillowcases per pillow as you have sets of sheets for the bed. Extra cases are nice if you like changing to a fresh one in the middle of a sweltering summer night.

3. **Mattress pad.** One per bed is the minimum for comfort and to protect your mattresses from wear and tear. If you stock an extra pad in the linen closet, you'll be able to strip and remake your bed from the mattress up without rushing to do the laundry first.

4. **Blankets.** Keep at least one warm winter blanket per bed and one lighter or thermal blanket for the summer. If you don't own a comforter or heavy quilt, stock a couple of extra blankets per bed.

5. **Duvet.** Duvets are also known as down comforters. They're optional, but wonderful on cool or cold nights because they are very light, yet extremely warm. They don't have to be made of down: lightweight silk or hypoallergenic synthetics are another option. They also come in light, medium, and winter weights. Choose yours based on the climate you live in and your preference for using it year-round, or only on cold nights. If you do invest in a comforter, buy a duvet cover to protect it.

 **FOR THE BATH**

Since you use them every single day, large and absorbent bath towels can make a significant contribution to your quality of life. Thicker towels will also be around long after skimpy and skinny bargain towels go threadbare.

1. **Bath towels.** You need a minimum of two per person in the household.

2. **Washcloths.** Buy washcloths to match the towels you purchase, even if not everyone in your household uses them. When you have to put out towels for house guests, you'll have more complete sets to choose from.

3. **Hand towels.** Follow the same principle as with towels and washcloths.

4. **Fingertip or hand towels for guests.** Stock at least three or four smaller towels for guests' use so you can rotate clean towels in. You can get by with decorative paper hand towels in a powder room, but cotton or linen is a nice touch. Fresh hand towels are essential when guests use the family bathroom.

5. **Bath mat.** Keep two bath mats per bathroom so they can be changed at least once a week.

6. **Bathroom rug.** Keep two per bathroom so one can be laundered while the other is in use.

Tip Stack complete sets of linens together, rather than storing separate stacks of pillow cases and sheets. Label your closet shelves with bed sizes to save the trouble of pulling out and opening the wrong sized sheet set.

A Sewing Kit for Basic Repairs

If you wouldn't know a bobbin from a bobby pin, and you visit your tailor more often than your mother across town, this list is for you. When a winter coat suddenly pops a button, or the heel of a shoe yanks out the hem of a skirt, where do you turn? You just open up that old cookie tin you prudently stocked with the following:

1. **Package of needles** in assorted sizes.

2. **Thread** in basic colors like white, black, beige, red, yellow, navy. You might want to add a spool of any other color you keep in your wardrobe (light blue, pink, purple, etc.).

3. **Thimble.** These are little metal helmets for your ring finger—the one that does battle with the needle you push through the fabric you're sewing. They help a lot.

4. **Needle threader.** If your eyesight isn't what it used to be, your hands are less than steady, or if you must thread an impossibly small needle, you'll be glad you have a needle threader. This flexible steel wire has a diamond-shaped opening that's easy to thread, and collapses when you push it through the needle's eye.

5. **Sharp scissors for cutting thread.** A single-edged razor blade can do the job, too, but it's a little more dangerous to have floating around in the kit.

6. **Extra buttons.** All those buttons that come with new clothes belong in here. You may even want to keep them in a separate container within or near the sewing box so the right button will be easier to find when you need it.

7. **Safety pins.** Think of safety pins as the duct tape of the sewing world. Use them for temporary repairs when you suddenly discover a drooping hem or a missing button on your skirt. Keep a few mid-sized pins and several of the tiny gold safety pins for these and other quick fixes.

8. **Mending and hemming tape.** This iron-on ad-hesive is a godsend for needle-and-thread phobics who must occasionally apply a patch, mend a tear, or fasten a hem. With this tape you can make a quick fix with nothing more than a hot iron.

 A Reference Library

Few things are as frustrating as needing the answer to a fairly straightforward question—Who directed *Shane?* Where is Mozambique? Who said "a foolish consistency is the hobgoblin of little minds?"—and not being able to find the answer quickly without calling the public library or firing up your computer. When you've got the right books on your reference shelf, the answers you need are at your fingertips. Here are the standard reference books you'll reach for again and again:

1. **Dictionary.** Take a look at the copyright date of the dictionary on your shelf. If you'd be suspicious of any can in your pantry with this date, it's time for a new edition. An older dictionary may be serviceable, but it won't include the most contemporary words and meanings, up-to-date biographical and geographical entries, or current acceptable usage, leaving you more open to making mistakes. See the box below for what to look for in your new dictionary.

2. **Thesaurus.** It's best not to depend exclusively on the thesaurus in your word processing system. Whether you're reaching for the best word to capture your meaning, or just want to limber up your vocabulary, an actual (as opposed to virtual) thesaurus will give you more words and more nuances of meaning to choose from. Look for a thesaurus that lists words alphabetically, so they're easier to find, and that groups synonyms according to similar meanings, so you choose the best word for the context.

3. **Book of quotations.** Look for a thorough collection of quotes—the bigger the book, the more likely it is to include that quote you're trying to track down. The books that are easiest to use are arranged

by subject, rather than author or chronology; subject listings allow easier browsing for just the right quote to use in a speech, and all good quote books include author indexes in case you know who said the quote you want. Look for a keyword index as well, so you can look up a quote you know even if you don't know the speaker or how it would be classified by subject.

4. **Atlas.** An up-to-date atlas—including the latest changes in country names, for example—is an invaluable tool. Large-format books make map reading easier, but come with high price tags; depending on how you'll use your atlas, a smaller, less pricey book may work for you.

5. **Video/movie guide.** Look for the most recent book with the largest number of movies and with cross-referencing of major producers, directors, and actors.

6. **Almanac.** Most almanacs are annuals, meant to be replaced every year. Look at a few different brands to find the book that displays information the way you prefer, and one with a complete index rather than a "concise" or "mini" index that does not cover the whole book.

7. **Classic all-purpose cookbook.** If your cookbook library is limited, choose a book with some basic kitchen how-to, such as how many minutes to cook an artichoke or how to carve a chicken, rather than one with recipes only.

8. **Household maintenance and repair handbook.** Unless you're a dedicated do-it-yourselfer, a general book will assist you with almost any home repair.

9. **Encyclopedia.** Select an encyclopedia based on the way you plan to use it. For most family reference fact-checking, a good one-volume encyclopedia is enough. Multivolume encyclopedias take up

shelf space and cost a bundle; a one-volume book is easier on the budget and can be replaced more often to keep your library up-to-date.

10. **Family medical encyclopedia.** Choose a book that allows you to look up symptoms, to help you avoid unnecessary trips to your physician.

11. **Etiquette book.** This may seem quaint or unnecessary, but next time you need to RSVP for a formal event or write a condolence note, you'll be glad you have an authoritative guide.

12. **Gardening book.** Be sure to choose one geared to your climate zone.

CHOOSING A DICTIONARY Dictionaries, like people, have different personalities. Keep this in mind when you're in search of the right one for your reference shelf. Think about the way you plan to use your dictionary to help you decide which features are important to you. Here are some things to consider:

Copyright date. Get the latest date available.

Number of definitions. This can vary by more than fifty thousand words.

New words. Look for terms like *road rage* and *intranet* if staying current with contemporary words is important to you.

Clear definitions. Some dictionaries list the most common meanings first, so the word you want is easier to find; others list meanings in historical order, so you may need to wade through some obsolete (but interesting!) meanings to find what you had in mind. Make sure definitions are clearly written and easy to understand. Compare by looking up the same word in each dictionary you are considering.

Extras. A good dictionary will be several books in one, including charts and tables, maps, grammar and usage tips, and other ready references. What extras would be most helpful to you?

Specific terms. Check to see if a dictionary is up-to-date on terms in technology, law, business, or other fields important to you.

Language usage. Look for a dictionary with clear notes on usage of commonly misused words. You may also want a book that clearly labels sensitive terms to help you avoid language that can be considered offensive. If you don't want your family to use a dictionary with sensitive language, look for a smaller book or one designed for family use that does not include these terms.

Home Maintenance

One of the toughest aspects of home maintenance—beyond the cost and hassle factor—is just remembering what to do when. Even simple and inexpensive (but vital) tasks may be neglected because no light goes on, nothing comes in the mail, and no one calls to remind us that we should, for example, drain and turn off outdoor water faucets in late fall or inspect and caulk windows in early spring. Now you have these checklists to help. All you have to do is remember to look at them!

Fall Maintenance Checklist

Squirrels do it, birds do it—and you should do it too: make your nest warm, safe, and snug before the chills of winter set in.

OUTSIDE THE HOUSE

1. **Prune tree branches** that touch the house.
2. **Clean rain gutters** and install wire strainers (to save yourself the trouble next year).

3. **Clean and store outdoor furniture.**

4. **Remove window screens.**

5. **Put up storm windows.**

6. **Check windows** for needed putty, weather stripping, or caulking.

7. **Inspect roof** for loose or missing shingles.

8. **Check chimney** for cracks, damaged bricks, loose flashing.

9. **Drain outside faucets** and hoses, put away hoses, and turn off faucets.

10. **Double-check drainage** (during rainstorm) to ensure water flows away from house.

> **Tip** To check for drafts, try the "hair dryer and candle test." One person blows a hair dryer at door and window crevices while a second watches the flame of a burning candle on the other side. You'll need to install weather stripping or caulk the edges of doors and windows where the flame flickered (or blew out!).

Inside the House

1. **Fill and clean humidifier,** test, and start.

2. **Have heating system checked** by serviceperson.

3. **Check area around furnace** and sweep away dust and flammable debris.

4. **Install clean air filter** and purchase several ahead of time, if you have the disposable type.

5. **Check chimney** for bird nests; hire chimney sweep if needed.

6. **Test fireplace damper.** It should open and close smoothly.

And Don't Forget . . .

Beat the crowds by stocking up on these items *before* the first big storm is predicted.

- Snow shovel
- Salt or chemical ice melting crystals
- Firewood
- Interior and exterior doormats that can handle mud and slush
- And . . . just to be safe, double-check the family cars for winter supplies (see page 277, "What to Carry in Your Car").

Spring Maintenance Checklist

When those first crocuses appear above the soil and visions of barbecues and bathing suits begin to dance in your head, pull out this checklist. It will help you locate any winter damage that needs attention and guide you in preparing your home for the warmer season.

 OUTSIDE THE HOUSE

1. **Remove and store storm windows.**

2. **Repair and install window screens.**

3. **Recheck caulking** around doors and windows.

4. **Inspect porch, steps, driveway, patio,** and any other concrete surfaces for cracks.

5. **Inspect wood deck** for:
   - wood rot (especially underneath crawl spaces and anywhere wood touches the ground)
   - loose or warped boards
   - cracks in railing
   - loose connections between railings or supports and main structure
   - water protection (if a glass of water soaks into the wood immediately instead of beading on the surface, apply water sealer or wood preservative)

6. **Inspect walls and painted surfaces** for cracks, peeling paint, and rot.

7. **Clean out rain gutters** if needed.

8. **Check flashing around chimney,** dormers, vents, and skylights.

9. **Look for loose or missing shingles** on roof.

10. **Open up and air out basement** when the weather is warm enough.

11. **Get barbecue** out of storage and clean it

Inside the House

1. **Shut off humidifier,** clean, drain.

2. **Inspect air conditioner,** test and call for repair if necessary.

3. **Reverse baffles in heating/air conditioning system** so cool air will flow to upper floors.

The Do-It-Yourselfer's Toolkit

Think of your toolbox as the first aid kit for your home. You'll keep your house "healthy" and save yourself both time and money if you're prepared to tackle at least the smaller jobs on your own. Here's advice from a Home Depot tool expert on what to buy and approximately how much to spend on each item.

 ## THE BASICS

1. **Hammer.** Heft a few until you find one that feels comfortable in your hand and seems to have a good balance when you raise it to swing. If you choose a wooden-handled hammer, look for a cast, rather than forged, steel claw. A 16-ounce weight claw hammer will probably be most comfortable for men; women often prefer a 12-ounce size. Expect to pay between $9 and $20.

2. **Pliers.** Pliers come in many varieties, and deciding which you need for your toolkit can be confusing. Start by getting the following four pairs, and you'll be armed for most challenges that call for pliers:
   - Standard pliers, sometimes known as pump pliers and sometimes referred to by a common brand name, Channel-Lock. Use these for plumbing work, tightening bolts, etc. (For larger plumbing jobs, see adjustable wrenches below.)
   - Needle-nose pliers. They're commonly used to hold wire in electrical work, so to be extra safe, buy a pair with an insulated handle (but never use them, or any other tool, on live wires).
   - Heavy duty cutters. These can cut bolts and screws as well as thicker sheets of metal.
   - Wire cutters. These will cut wire and thinner pieces of metal.

You can pick up a good pair of pliers for around $5 apiece—less if you buy a packaged set. Choose a tool that feels comfortable in your hand, but generally a pair about 8 inches long will work well for assorted tasks.

3. **Adjustable wrench.** These wrenches, commonly referred to by the brand name, Crescent wrench, open and close to the size of the item you're turning. They'll open up very wide to accommodate larger pipes. A good-quality wrench that's easy to grip should go for $15 to $20.

4. **Screwdrivers.** You'll want a variety of these, including one or two cheap ones for dirty jobs like opening paint cans. The easiest way to make sure you always have what you need is to buy a set of four: a large and small flat and a large and small Phillips head. Look for a one- and two-point Phillips and a 1/4-inch and a 3/16-inch flat. You can even get a single handle package with interchangeable heads for $15 or less. You'll also find a surprising number of uses for one of those tiny screwdrivers used for repairing eyeglasses. They come in handy for jobs on cabinet hinges, towel bars, childproofing devices, and, well . . . eyeglasses.

5. **Cross-cut saw.** Also called a hand or ripping saw. As the name suggests, this tool cuts across the grain and is the basic saw you'll use for most projects. Choose one with eight teeth to the inch and expect to pay about $20.

6. **Hacksaw or close-quarter hacksaw.** This is a C-shaped saw generally used to cut metal (as in pipes). Look for one that costs about $8.

7. **Miter saw.** This saw cuts at an angle, making it ideal for cutting molding or other angled wood cuts about an inch or less. It should be roughly the same price as the hacksaw.

8. **Electric drill.** If you get a cordless drill, you're ready for anything—including making repairs when a storm has knocked the power out. Plug-in models are less expensive and generally more heavy-duty. Figure on spending about $40 for the cordless and $10 less for the traditional drill, plus another $10 for a set of starter bits.

9. **Plunger.** Although these are known as plumber's friends, using one can save you from lining your plumber's pockets. It's a good idea to keep a small plunger for unstopping sinks and a larger one exclusively for toilets. They cost around $6 each.

10. **Utility knife with razor blades.** These are invaluable for scraping paint from windows, opening boxes, cutting wallpaper or carpeting, and a variety of other jobs. Get one with a pointed edge to use for boxes and one flat push type with a retractable blade for scraping. Expect to spend only a few dollars on each.

OTHER SMALL BUT HANDY ITEMS TO KEEP IN YOUR TOOLKIT

1. **Measuring tape,** 16-foot metal.

2. **Picture hangers** and wall anchors (for hanging heavy items such as large mirrors or paintings).

3. **Glue gun.** If you don't already have one, pick up this handy device. Chances are you'll be keeping it within easy reach for help with everything from broken crockery to craft projects. About $5 at hardware or craft stores.

4. **All-purpose glue (such as Elmer's) and super glue.** If you just want to make a quick repair and don't want to bother heating up a glue gun, keep a tube of each handy.

5. **Pencil and eraser.** For marking (and unmarking) your measurements. Erasers are also great for removing small scuff and scratch marks from painted walls.

6. **Putty-knife and hole-filling compound.** The type of filling material you need will depend on what kind of walls you have (plaster, drywall, etc.).

7. **Sand sponges.** These are good for smaller sanding jobs because they're much easier to grip and use than sandpaper. As a plus, they can be washed and reused.

8. **Miscellaneous screws, washers, bolts, etc.** These are sometimes called assortment boxes and come in clear plastic containers. Look around your house first to see what size you're most likely to need. An assortment tray that's 6×6 inches, ½–¾-inch high with six to ten compartments should come with everything you need to do from hanging your kindergartner's art to fixing a wobbly table.

9. **Two-foot level.** This plastic device will tell you whether you're hanging pictures and mirrors straight and also help you get vertical plumb lines—and it will fit in your toolbox. You only need a level longer than two feet if you expect to be working on larger projects.

10. **Pair of C-clamps.** For holding items together while you nail, glue, or screw them, C-clamps can be better than an extra set of hands.

11. **Card of thumbtacks.** A thumbtack is perfect for temporarily holding something to wall since it makes only a tiny hole. For installing picture hangers, drapery hardware blinds, and so forth, use thumbtacks to mark the spot and then use that as the starter hole.

12. **Duct and masking tape.** Use duct tape for emergency situations until the final repair can be set in

place. If a window is shattered but not broken, duct or masking tape will hold it together. Mend torn window screens, cover drafty cracks under windows, or use these tapes for any other job that needs to be done immediately, but must wait for a permanent repair. Masking tape is also useful for labeling boxes and shielding areas you're painting around.

13. **Electrical tape.** This is used for making capped wire connections watertight. Never connect wires with electrical tape alone because the wires won't be insulated and electrocution is very possible.

14. **Assortment of wire nuts.** These are plastic caps in multicolors, coded for size. Red ones are large, yellow are medium, blue are smaller. Have an assortment at hand for connecting and insulating all sizes of wire.

Tip Should you buy the best tool you can afford or just get by with an inexpensive one? Let your size, strength, skill, and ambition level be your guide. Denise Whitacre, home repair and maintenance specialist for Home Depot, says expensive tools that provide longer-term durability are needed mainly by professionals or homeowners who plan to add rooms or do extensive renovations. She puts it this way: "Why buy King Kong when Cheetah will do?"

✓ Tricks of the Trade: How to Avoid Calling a Repairman

Things fall apart. They also get clogged, jammed, broken, or just mysteriously stop working—usually when you can least afford the disruption. Instead of calling a repairman (they rarely come quickly—or cheaply), try these fix-it-yourself methods for a few common household predicaments.

1. To unclog sinks and tubs:
- Remove as much standing water as possible and slowly pour a large pot of boiling water down the drain to dissolve the blockage.
- Pump the drain three times with a plunger. Try a couple of times, if necessary.
- Put a bucket under the U-shaped part of the drain pipe and unscrew it with a wrench. Poke a bent wire hanger up toward the drain to dislodge the goop.
- Help keep drains clear by pouring a cup of bleach down every couple of weeks. Many plumbers discourage using chemical drain cleaners because they contain caustic chemicals which are dangerous, bad for the plumbing, and not particularly effective.

2. To fix stopped-up toilets:
- If something such as a child's toy or washcloth has accidentally fallen into the toilet, roll up your sleeves, pull on your rubber gloves, and fish around in there until you find it. To make longer "gloves," use a couple of old plastic bread wrappers fastened loosely around your upper arm with rubber bands.
- Don't flush. Let the water drain away as much as possible and pour in a bucket of boiling water all at once.

- Push a toilet plunger up and down as firmly and quickly as possible. Be sure the cup fits snugly over the bottom of the bowl. Repeat at least three times.
- Buy or rent a plumber's auger (a long snake with a metal spiral at the end). Push it into the bowl and keep cranking until it meets the blockage. At that point you can either try to pull the blockage out by slowly retracting the auger, or move the auger handle around quickly to dislodge the obstruction.

3. **To fix an electricity failure:** Electricity is something you don't want to fool around with casually, but some problems are simple to diagnose and correct. If you can't easily solve an electrical problem, call an expert—don't try to fix it yourself.

- In a blackout or partial blackout. Look outside to see if nearby homes have been affected. If not, grab a flashlight and check your circuit breakers to see if an overload has tripped them. You'll recognize this because the breakers will have moved away from the "on" position. If this has happened, first switch off all but a couple of lights and the refrigerator. Then turn on the breakers one by one. Turning breakers on all at once can blow your entire circuit box.
- If a lamp or room light won't work. Unscrew the light bulb and shake it gently. If you hear a tiny rattle, the filament is broken and the bulb must be replaced. If the bulb seems okay, twist it to see if it's screwed in properly. Bulbs sometimes work loose and just need to be tightened. Go to the circuit box and see if the circuit breaker has been tripped due to an overload. And don't overlook the "duh" factor—if there's a light switch on the wall, make sure it's in the on position.

4. To fix dripping water faucets:

- If you have a newer type of faucet, with hot and cold combined, you will probably need to replace the cartridge to fix a drip. Purchase a repair kit from a hardware store and follow the instructions.

- If you have a classic stem faucet with separate hot and cold handles, turn off the water supply, unscrew the handle, and replace the old washer with a new one from your toolbox (see page 00). If you don't have a new washer, you can sometimes make do by turning the old one over.

- If you prefer a quick fix to a permanent repair (at 3:00 A.M., perhaps), wrap a string around the spout and let it trail into the sink. The water will soak into the string and slip quietly into the sink. To conserve water, put a pan in the sink and save the leakage for your plants or garden.

5. To correct low flow from a faucet:

- This is sometimes caused by a buildup of deposits or small debris in the aerator (the little screen at the end of the spout). Unscrew the nozzle and clear out the screen.

- Occasionally, water flow is blocked by a worn washer at the spout. If the aerator screen is clean, inspect the washer for signs of wear.

6. To clear a jammed garbage disposal:

- Before removing an item from the disposal, *always* make sure the wall switch is turned off. Remove the black-flapped washer from the top of the disposal and retrieve the loose item from the bottom. When the item is out, run the cold water, push the small red button at the bottom of the machine to reset the circuit breaker, then flip the wall switch on. If the machine still doesn't work, try resetting the circuit breaker again.

- To remove an item that can't be retrieved by simply reaching in from the top, insert a disposal wrench (available in any hardware store) into the hole at the bottom of the unit and rotate the wrench back and forth to free the disposal blades. If you don't have a disposal wrench, try inserting a broom handle into the business end of the unit and gently working the teeth around until you can pull the object free. Then follow the procedure above for resetting the circuit breaker.

- Keep the disposal clean and sanitary by grinding ice cubes in it every couple of weeks and adding a few tablespoons of Comet (or other powdered cleanser with bleach) while the unit runs.

☑ How to Hire a Contractor or Roofer

Remodeling and reroofing are among the largest cash outlays you will make on your home. And if you make a mistake in hiring, you may do serious damage to your home, your finances, and your nerves. The secret to getting a job done well and on budget is to find a professional with a succession of happy clients to his name and then check him out as if he were proposing to your daughter. Here's how:

1. **Get referrals.** Ask family and friends who've had work done on their houses for names of professionals they were satisfied with. If another professional such as a decorator or architect recommends someone, go see that contractor's work before you call for an appointment.

2. **Check references.** This is a no-brainer, or at least it should be. But you'd be surprised at the number of people who ask for references but never check a single one. No matter how confident you feel about the person, don't skip this step! Even clients who were generally satisfied with a contractor's work may give you useful tips about working with that particular contractor.

3. **Check with local officials.** Call the city building code inspector and your local builder's or roofer's licensing agency to find out what licenses a contractor is required to have. Also ask what special permits are needed to perform the job you're planning. Find out who is responsible for providing workman's compensation. Whether the responsibility lies with you, the contractor, or the subcontractor varies by locality. While you're on the phone, check to see if any complaints have been lodged against the professionals you are considering.

4. **Check credentials.** Now that you know precisely what's required, ask to see the contractor's proof of license, insurance, and bonding. If this person plans to use subcontractors, ask for their credentials as well. Ask if the contractor plans to pull the necessary permits for your job. Never allow a contractor to wink-and-nudge you into doing the job without the required permits.

5. **Listen to intuition.** It's not enough to make sure your contractor has all his papers in order. Equally important is how you feel about the person who will have virtual dominion over your household for some time to come. How are this person's manners and attitude? Does he return your calls promptly and show up for appointments on time? If you're less than certain about the contractor you're considering, keep looking. It will be much less trouble to continue your search than it will to survive days, weeks, or months of frustration and torment at the hands of a problem professional.

6. **Ask for an itemized bid.** It's self-preservation, not nit-picking, to insist on a detailed bid, specifying the exact materials (down to the kind of nails) the contractor will use. The bid should also contain a step-by-step plan for performing the work and an estimate of labor costs. Labor prices will vary according to locality and among different contractors, but expect the total for labor to be about 15 percent more than the costs for materials.

7. **Get it in writing.** After you've chosen a contractor, protect yourself with a carefully written contract. Assume nothing and never sign a blank or incomplete document. Indicate with words and pictures exactly what work is to be done. If it's a roofing job, will the original roof be removed? How many layers? Who is liable for protecting your property if it rains while the roof is off?

8. **Name the dates.** One of the most important items on your contract (especially for your peace of mind) will be the date the work is to commence and the date by which it must be complete. Use dates, not number of working days. This way, if your contractor drags his feet on getting started, you have the opportunity to choose someone else for the job.

9. **Include a payment schedule.** This portion of the contract states that the contractor will be paid for materials as they are purchased and used. If you pay as you go and the contractor can't or won't complete the work, you'll still have money (or materials) to finish the job. Make it clear that you want to see receipts for all materials purchased for your project. Spell out the percentage amount by which the total cost of the job might overrun the estimate (10 to 15 percent is a common amount).

10. **Watch those warranties.** A contractor's warranty usually covers his work only. A manufacturer's warranty covers materials separately, and frequently limits liability in cases where the manufacturer's instructions for use are not followed. Make sure you understand these warranties and discuss them with your contractor. Then write the details into your contract.

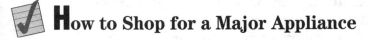

How to Shop for a Major Appliance

Whether you're about to purchase your first washing machine or replace an ancient refrigerator, buying a major appliance can be nerve wracking. These modern conveniences cost a large chunk of change and they're built to last a long time, so the pressure to buy the right item can make even a seasoned homeowner feel apprehensive. Here's how to approach the job with a bit more confidence.

1. **Focus on features.** As soon as you know you're "in the market" for an appliance, begin thinking about what features are important to you. Do a reality check by talking to friends who have similar appliances. Ask your friends if the icemaker on their refrigerator has given them trouble and whether the chilled water dispenser was worth the extra expense. Discuss the fine points of microwave cooking and talk about large- versus small-capacity dishwashers. Ask for their opinions on the best location for a dryer's lint trap. You may not agree with their preferences, but at least you'll have a more educated opinion about your ideal appliance.

2. **Do the numbers.** Determine how much you want to spend on the appliance and then decide how you'd prefer to pay for it. If you're going to buy on credit, you may want to make favorable financing terms a significant factor in your decision on where to buy.

3. **Shop in the 'hood.** Local retailers who must compete with national chains can be great places to shop because they depend on word-of-mouth and repeat business for their survival. The salespeople are likely to have more time to devote to customers

and to be knowledgeable about the products they sell. Smaller stores make themselves as attractive as possible by offering whatever they can afford; sometimes this means lower prices, more often it will be superior customer service or comfortable financing terms.

4. **Weigh price against store extras.** While you're deciding where to shop, take into account services that can affect the ultimate cost of your purchase. For example, a higher-priced refrigerator that comes with free delivery may be cheaper in the long run than another retailer's discount fridge that comes with a hefty delivery charge. It's also a good idea to ask about the store's policy on installation, follow-up servicing, delayed or low-interest financing, and other extras that could lower the total amount.

5. **Stick with the standards.** In most cases, you'll be better off buying appliances with established brand names. This doesn't mean that you should base your choice on whether or not the name rings a bell. But it does suggest you may have a better experience with an appliance from a maker known for reliability. The product may also be easier to repair when the time comes because parts—and knowledgeable repair people—are easier to find.

6. **Try for a trade-in.** If you are replacing an existing appliance, you may be able to get credit for your older model. This is another area in which you may find more flexibility with a local merchant than with a national chain.

7. **Give it an audition.** Whenever possible, ask to see the product in action. This will help you gauge actual performance against your expectations and will allow you to decide if it's easy to use (ask the salesperson to let you operate the controls).

8. **Read the fine print.** It won't make the best-seller list, but the warranty on the product you're considering is definitely a good thing to read. Take time to study it and understand what the manufacturer promises to cover and for how long.

9. **Know when to walk away.** At some stores, only after you agree to buy the product do you get the real sales pitch. Salespeople are trained to make extended warranties (sometimes called service contracts) sound like a mighty good deal. And they usually are—for the store. Consider these contracts only if you know you'll be giving the appliance a much harder or more frequent workout than the typical user.

Housework and Other Emergencies

We all like a clean house. It's getting there that isn't any fun at all. Most of us would just as soon get it out of the way as quickly as possible—and with the minimum of effort. These checklists will make sure you know what to do, and have the right materials to make the job easier.

✓ **B**are Minimum Housework: From Pigsty to Presentable in Six Steps

Okay, so you had a busy week. You worked late every night and left your take-out food cartons around, tossed mail aside after opening it, dropped newspapers and magazines after reading them, and abandoned several items of clothing where you stepped out of them. And you haven't vacuumed, dusted, or cleaned the bathroom in two weeks. The place looks more like a frat house after a party than the abode of a hardworking, career-minded adult—whose friend suddenly calls from the airport and says she's coming by in five minutes.

1. **Close the door!** The whole point of bare minimum housework is to do only what's immediately necessary. Decide which rooms and areas of your

home will be on view and focus your energy and attention there. Don't forget the bathroom—and any rooms leading to it. In a true housework emergency, any door that shuts and won't be opened can be your best friend.

2. **Attack clutter.** Make a rapid circuit, picking up newspapers, tennis shoes, books, vases of dead flowers, soccer balls, pizza cartons—anything that doesn't belong. It's a good idea to do this with a trash bag in one hand and a box or laundry basket in the other. Fill the trash bag as you go and pile miscellaneous items into the basket for tossing behind those closed doors.

3. **Dust.** After tidying, dusting gives you the biggest bang for your cleaning buck. Grab a soft cloth, or feather or lamb's wool duster, and start at the top, working down. The job will go much faster if you move lamps, telephones, framed pictures, etc., off tables and other surfaces before you start. When surfaces are clean, dust and wipe smudges off lamps and decorative items before replacing them.

4. **Fluff and straighten.** Now that your furniture is visible, with clutter and dust cleared, make the room look inviting. Fluff throw pillows, straighten slipcovers, arrange knick-knacks, and stack books and magazines attractively.

5. **Vacuum or nitpick.** If there's time, run the vacuum. If not, pick up smaller throw rugs and shake them outside, then pick any obvious lint, threads, dead plant leaves, etc., off the carpet. If you have hardwood floors, go to the areas where dust bunnies collect (in corners, under tables, behind doors), and scoop them up with a damp paper towel.

6. **Speed-scrub the bathroom.** Cleaning a bathroom can be done quickly, no matter how grim the

room looks when you begin. First, stow everything you can in a cabinet or medicine chest: move the toothpaste, makeup, shaving cream, and last week's mail out of sight. If you can get away with it, close the shower curtain or close the tub door and ignore the bathtub. Arm yourself with a pair of latex gloves, a bottle of liquid cleaner with bleach, a roll of paper towels, and a sponge. Douse the sink with liquid cleaner and pour about a quarter cup into the toilet. After the cleanser has steeped for a minute or two, wash the sink quickly, rinse it, and polish faucets, handles, and the medicine cabinet mirror with a damp paper towel. Scrub the toilet with a bowl brush, and use a wet sponge or paper towels to wipe dust and hair from the floor and base of the toilet. Keep wiping the floor as you back out of the room.

Cleaning Supplies

Music is the secret weapon in your cleaning arsenal. Before you pick up so much as a dust rag, go to the cabinet and pull out a rocking, hopping CD. It will boost your energy and put some rhythm into your mopping; or at the very least it will distract you from the drudgery. The best to be said for the rest of this stuff is that the right cleaning tools and potions will make the job easier and will allow you to keep pace with the music.

 ## CLEANING TOOLS

1. **Rubber gloves.** A sturdy pair will enable you to tackle jobs you might otherwise shrink from. They'll also keep your hands and nails from looking like you just spent the day, well, cleaning.

2. **Vacuum cleaner.** If you have allergies, invest in one with a Hepa filter. If you don't have the room to store an upright, buy the best canister style you can find.

3. **Sponge mop.** Buy one with a replaceable sponge head. Purchase a few replacements at a time so you can change them quickly when one wears out in the middle of a job.

4. **Feather dusters.** They may evoke images of French maids in frilly aprons, but these are serious work tools and can't be beat for quickly dusting many items at once, like books or knick-knacks.

5. **Dust cloths.** An old cotton dish towel or diaper is ideal. Or consider giving new life to old favorites by cutting T-shirts or flannel nightgowns down to duster size. Keep separate cloths for shining wood

furniture with polish and oils and for cleaning surfaces (like windows and walls) that should be oil-
free.

6. **Sponges.** A variety of sizes will be useful for different cleaning chores: wiping down woodwork and
countertops, cleaning out sinks, tubs, ovens, and so
forth. Buy a few combination sponge/scrubbers for
heavy-duty jobs like cleaning the oven and scrubbing the tub.

7. **Toilet brush with its own holder.** Do yourself
a favor and keep one behind each toilet in the
house. You'll find the job much easier to tackle
when all you need to do is whip the brush from its
holder and scrub, swish, shake, and stow.

8. **Plastic bucket.** This is essential for cleaning
floors, walls, or any other surface that calls for mixing cleaning solutions with water, or rinsing large
surfaces with water.

 ## CLEANING POTIONS

1. **Spray-on glass cleaner.** Use for cleaning windows, mirrors, pictures, and other glass surfaces.

2. **All-purpose liquid cleaner.** Use this for floors,
counters, or walls. But use it carefully (first spray on
the cloth, then wipe surface) so you don't remove
paint along with the fingerprints on walls and
woodwork. Consider purchasing a gentle formula
that is easy on paint and nontoxic to humans.

3. **Disinfectant.** If your all-purpose cleaner doesn't
contain a disinfectant, keep Lysol or a similar product on hand for sanitizing garbage cans, children's
play areas, or any surface where germs are a special
problem.

4. **Powdered cleanser.** Use it on toilets, sinks, and tubs, but never on paint or any surface that will scratch easily.

5. **Bleach.** It can work miracles removing mold and mildew in the bathroom. It can also save you unpleasant digging and scrubbing on discolored tile grouting. Pour on some bleach, let sit for a minute or two to loosen dirt or mildew, and rinse away. A few words of caution: Never use bleach around upholstered furniture or carpets and never wear anything that you wouldn't like to see decorated with white drip and splash marks. No matter how careful you think you're being, they *will* appear on your clothing. *Never mix bleach with ammonia. It will cause a toxic gas. Read product labels to be sure of contents.*

6. **Furniture polish.** A spray can is easy to use and helps capture the dust while leaving a glossy finish on furniture.

7. **Furniture oil.** It comes in dark or light and should be used frequently on open-grained (nonveneered) furniture to keep the wood gleaming and prevent drying and cracking.

✓ Checklist for Spring Cleaning

You might as well know the worst about housework. Every year about forty pounds of dust sneaks into your house and settles into every possible nook and cranny. The good news is that it doesn't arrive all at once and your regular housecleaning (however hasty) gets rid of some of it. The bad news is that the other thirty-eight pounds continue to lurk in less obvious places. Tracking down and scrubbing away this dirt is the annual rite known as Spring Cleaning. Here are some of the jobs you'll want to consider for your own Rites of Spring. *Warning:* Attempting to tackle items on this checklist all at once can be hazardous to your mental and physical health! Spread them over a few weekends, so you don't lose momentum *or* sanity.

1. **Wash windows.** Ideally, this should be done twice a year. It's easier to do the job with a partner who cleans one side of the window while you do the other, helping you spot streaks and smears right away. Don't forget to clean windowsills and the window wells that collect dead leaves and bugs.

2. **Clean window screens.** Remove screens and hose them down outside; use a stiff bristled brush if necessary.

3. **Wash or dry-clean drapes.**

4. **Wash shower curtain** with bleach and water mixture or buy a fresh curtain.

5. **Wash walls and woodwork** as needed.

6. **Shampoo carpets.**

7. **Have upholstered furniture professionally cleaned.** Don't forget throw pillows!

8. **Clean out clothes closets.** Donate or give away unused clothes, shoes, toys, or other items. Any-

thing you haven't worn in a year should go. (See page 40 on organizing your closet.)

9. **Clean and straighten the linen closet.**

10. **Clean out medicine cabinets.** Clean shelves and replace items that are used regularly. Discard expired medicines.

11. **Clean out kitchen cabinets.** Throw away expired food and wipe the interior. Change the shelf paper.

12. **Move large appliances.** Clean under and behind them. Vacuum dust from the front coil of the refrigerator (it's important to do this at least twice a year).

13. **Clean the refrigerator.** Empty it out and thoroughly clean shelves and walls of unit; reorganize items as you replace them.

14. **Clean the oven and stovetop.** If needed, take burners apart and scrub them.

15. **Go through bookshelves.** Remove books that can be donated, given away, or sold. Dust books and shelves with soft cloth.

16. **Clean ashes from fireplace.** Scrub hearth.

How to Do a Load of Laundry (So You'll Recognize It Afterward)

If this checklist looks like much ado about a pile of dirty clothes, don't be put off. Once you've washed and dried a few loads of laundry successfully, you'll be sorting, zipping, softening, and folding like an old pro and won't give another thought to the steps involved.

1. **Read labels.** Paying attention to the manufacturer's care instructions keeps your clothes looking better longer and (in some cases) will save them from instant death.

2. **Sort.** Separate darks from lights and regular care fabrics from delicates. Put fragile or small delicate items (like panty hose and lingerie) in a mesh bag before washing to protect them from snagging, tangling, and getting lost in the machine. Also, sort loads by how dirty they are and wash oily or greasy clothes separately.

3. **Check pockets.** Sometimes lurking pocket contents can make an annoying mess, leaving you to pick tiny bits of wet tissue off your black turtleneck. Sometimes they can do permanent damage, as anyone who's ever left a fountain pen in a pocket can attest.

4. **Close buttons and zippers.** This precaution keeps clothes from catching on parts of the machine or on each other, saving wear and tear on everything you wash.

5. **Treat stains.** Most of the stain removers on the market do a decent job of treating common stains. Be sure to treat the stain as soon as possible. (See "How to Remove Stains," page 94.)

6. **Set load level, fabric cycle, and water temperature.** Most washers allow you to choose all three: Water level (for small, medium, or large loads); fabric cycle (regular, delicate, permanent press); and water temperature.
   - Use hot or warm water for very dirty loads, but cooler or cold water on permanent press and colors.
   - Use warm water for white items that are not prone to shrinkage. Be careful with hot water, which can cause whites to yellow.
   - Read the labels on your clothes for laundering instructions. If there are none (or you've cut the labels off), keep in mind that eight minutes is the optimum duration for any wash cycle. Using a longer time setting even on really dirty clothes can actually redeposit soil on fabrics. Knits, sweaters, and delicate items need a shorter wash cycle, preferably one with gentle agitation.

7. **Measure detergent.** Use the quantity suggested on the container. Using too much detergent leaves a soapy residue; using too little leaves clothes dirty. Keep a plastic measuring cup with your laundry supplies.

8. **Add bleach.** Many fabric guides specify "nonchlorine bleach only," so stocking a nonchlorinated bleach is a good idea. You can also use it on fabrics that can survive chlorine bleach. If you do use bleach, always dilute it before adding it to the washer *and* be sure to let the machine fill completely and agitate for a few moments before adding laundry. If you skip this step, your towels, sheets, and T-shirts may be squeaky clean, but they'll look as if they've been nibbled by rodents (which spoils the dazzling white effect).

9. **Start washer.** Starting the machine and allowing the detergent to mix with the water before you add

the laundry is kinder to your things because it distributes the detergent evenly through the wash water. This is especially important when using powdered detergents, which can clump and leave stains if they haven't dissolved before the clothing is added.

10. **Add laundry and shut lid.** Many machines won't begin washing and none will spin dry until the door is closed. Once you've added the laundry and shut the lid, you're off duty for twenty-eight minutes or so.

11. **Dry clothes.** Unless you'd like to create a Lilliputian wardrobe, take a little extra time to separate out clothes that should be line dried or dried flat before you put the rest of the load in the dryer.

12. **Toss in fabric softener sheet.** These are easy to use and require little more of you than buying a package and opening the box. One sheet in a normal load will reduce wrinkling and static.

13. **Remove clothes promptly.** If you hate to iron, do yourself a favor and hang or fold your clothes as soon as they are dry.

How to Remove Stains

The best advice for removing a stain from any surface is to treat it immediately if at all possible. Before applying any strong solution, such as lighter fluid or nail polish remover, first test an inconspicuous section of the fabric. Here are some of the most common kinds of stains and a few remedies.

1. **Blood.** Rinse with cold water right away; if the stain remains, sprinkle it with meat tenderizer and cool water. Rinse with cool water after twenty minutes. If the blood has dried, brush away excess so the stain won't spread when you dissolve it.

2. **Candle wax.** Sprinkle corn starch or talcum powder on the spot and cover with a paper towel. Press gently with a warm iron. If color from the candle remains, spray with stain remover and let sit for five to ten minutes before washing.

3. **Chewing gum.** Freeze the gum with an ice cube and break the gum from the fabric. If a stain remains, rub gently with full-strength detergent and wash.

4. **Chocolate.** Blot or scrape off excess, rinse the fabric with cold water, then rub with full-strength detergent and rinse again with cool water. If the stain remains, apply a fifty-fifty vinegar and water solution and blot. If the stain still remains, blot with lighter fluid or weak bleach solution and launder as usual.

5. **Coffee.** Treat the same as chocolate stains.

6. **Fruit juice.** Rinse under cold water. If the stain remains, rub with the cut side of a lemon. But test carefully first, because lemon is "nature's bleach."

7. **Grass stains.** Rub with liquid detergent or try slightly diluted hydrogen peroxide or bleach (if the fabric can take it).

8. **Ink.** Many experts suggest spraying with hair spray and blotting. You may also try pouring salt on an ink stain while it's still wet, or sponging it with water and applying a mixture of liquid detergent and a few drops of vinegar.

9. **Oil** (including grease, butter and salad dressing). Wash with detergent and hot water and rinse. For more delicate fabrics, try club soda. Use corn starch to absorb the grease on rough textured fabrics, let it sit overnight; if the stain remains, try the detergent and hot water method.

10. **Wine.** Club soda is the standard remedy for red wine stains. If the stain remains after blotting with soda, sprinkle with salt and let sit for fifteen minutes, then wash with cold water and cold-water detergent.

Flowers and Plants: Checklists for Brown Thumbs

When Kermit, that Muppet philosopher, observes, "It isn't easy being green," he could be talking plants as easily as frogs. Many of us struggle to keep our greenery thriving, but often find we're doing it serious damage instead. These lists will get you started on a beautiful garden, indoors or out.

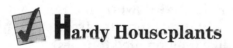 **Hardy Houseplants**

Placing a few green plants around your home or office can brighten any room dramatically. But it only takes one or two droopy or brown plants to quickly achieve the opposite effect. If this is a familiar scenario, take heart. The key to consistently flourishing flora lies in selecting plants that can survive the conditions you're able to provide. This may mean choosing plants that prefer low light, or sticking with plants that don't insist on regular watering, if you're forgetful. Here are eight hardy plants and a few suggestions about supplying their modest needs.

1. **Aloe** *(Aloe barbadensis)*. Also known as the medicine plant because aloe helps soothe and heal burns, this graceful, long-armed succulent is a good choice for the kitchen. Wise cooks rub its sticky (and stinky) juice on burns. Aloe is about as low-maintenance as they come, but does need good light. Since it's a member of the cactus family, you can let it go without water until it's positively parched, then water sparingly.

2. **Cast iron plant** *(Aspidistra elatior)*. This plant's name alone should gladden the heart of even the most timid gardener. The cast iron plant has even been praised in song; "The Biggest Aspidistra in the World" is a testament to its wild popularity in the Victorian era and its habit of steady growth under all conditions. It has oblong, dark-green leaves that are long and pointed at the ends. The leaves arc outward from spears rising directly from the soil. It can serve as a demure table plant, or can be encouraged (with light, fertilizer, and ever-larger pots) to grow into a gargantuan specimen worthy of its song.

3. **Chinese evergreen** *(Aglaonema* 'silver queen'*)*. This easygoing plant will tolerate downright dim light, but can also thrive in direct sun. Its silvery green leaves look a bit like long pointed tongues and sprout from short stems, giving the medium-sized floor plant a bushy or shrublike appearance. Keep it out of drafts and water when the soil surface is dry, and the Chinese evergreen will brighten your dark corners for many years.

4. **Ficus** *(Ficus benjamina)*. Sometimes called the weeping fig, this popular indoor plant is a staple of offices and living rooms. The graceful ficus has an undeserved reputation as a temperamental plant because sometimes it will "mysteriously" drop every leaf from its pale wood branches. There isn't a mystery,

really. The tree has been keeping a stiff upper lip under poor conditions for months or even years, and has finally used up its reserves. The ficus is the most "high maintenance" plant on this list, but its needs are simple: Give it good light, water moderately when it's dry, and don't move it unless absolutely necessary. Pop one of those fertilizer stakes into the soil and replace when necessary. With a little care, *Ficus benjamina* will grow slowly but steadily for years.

5. **Golden pothos** *(Epipremnum aureum)*. If you are a forgetful waterer, this creamy yellow- and green-leafed plant is for you. Pothos likes to be drenched periodically and to dry out completely in between. It thrives in bright light (no direct sun), but can exist in shaded areas. With abundant light, pothos will grow quickly, but it tolerates cramped roots, so you needn't repot it constantly. You can grow it large and use as a floor plant to fill in a lonely corner, or display it on a table, or in a hanging basket. Pinch new growth every now and then to encourage fullness. If it starts to look leggy or unhappy, just cut it way back and your pothos will become full and healthy all over again.

6. **Mother-in-law's tongue** *(Sansevieria trifasciata)*. This virtually indestructible plant got its popular name because of its long, sharp leaves. (You can tell your mother-in-law it is a snake plant, another common nickname.) Along with its cactus cousins, the snake plant prefers to stay fairly dry and likes abundant light. But it has been known to thrive in dim rooms and sometimes goes for as long as six weeks without water. Its deep-green leaves extend gracefully upward and it can grow from several inches to several feet high.

7. **Split-leaf philodendron** *(Philodendron bipennifolium)*. The split-leaf looks nothing like its larger

cousin, the tree philodendron. But the two have a few important qualities in common: a general toughness and tolerance for low light and infrequent watering. Its leaves start out tender and pale green but turn deep green and leathery, splitting into sections, as it grows. Water when the soil surface is dry. If it begins to look unhealthy, cut it back to the soil and give the roots a good soaking; the plant will reward your minimal efforts by starting all over again.

8. **Tree philodendron** *(Philodendron bipinnatifidum)*. Its large leaves are deeply cut in an almost frond- or fingerlike pattern and, as its name suggests, it makes a good floor plant. In fact, tree philodendrons are ideal for low-light areas where you want to fill in a bare spot and will grow very large if you keep repotting to larger containers. This plant will thrive under the absent-minded gardener, since it likes to be drenched and to dry out between binges.

✓ First Aid for Dying Plants

The secret to keeping plants alive is to recognize what's killing them and fix it fast. This checklist describes the most common houseplant killers, helps you recognize symptoms, and explains how to apply a remedy before it's too late.

1. **Overwatering.** This is the single most common cause of death for houseplants and generally happens for one of two reasons. Most often, we're overly affectionate, giving plants too much of what they need. Sometimes, we're overly efficient, regularly, but lethally, giving every plant the same amount of water on the same schedule.

   Symptoms. The earliest symptom of overwatering may be as obvious as puddles in the plant saucer. One of the most reliable—but less easy to recognize—signs that you've been killing your plant with kindness is a generalized yellowing of the leaves. Sometimes the leaf tips turn black and the yellow leaves fall. As the damage progresses, your plant may sprout brown to black fungal spots on the yellow leaves. If you've turned a blind eye to all of this, the plant will eventually collapse and die because its entire root system has rotted away. A foul odor in the plant mix is another sign that the roots are rotting.

   Cures. If you've overwatered your plant on a single occasion, just pour off any standing water, allow the soil to dry out again, and the plant will be fine. But if you notice advanced symptoms, you'll need to give it some help drying out. Gently inspect the soil and roots; if the soil is especially mushy and the plant has a reasonably well-established root system, lift it out and put the root ball directly on a stack of newspapers, which will draw out the moisture. If the plant is young, or not that wet, just put the pot (which, of course, has a drainage hole in the bottom!) on newspapers and change them as needed. After drying the plant, disinfect the pot to get rid of any accumulated fungus; otherwise the roots may rot again, however carefully you water.

How much is too much? Most plants like to be watered when the soil is dry about a third of the way down the pot. You can buy a plant meter at the nursery, but any of the low-tech methods like twisting a pencil or your finger deep into the soil will also be a fairly reliable indicator of the moisture level. But check the instructions that come on the plant, or ask the expert at the store if the plant you're buying has special watering requirements.

2. **Underwatering.** This can happen if you're away on vacation, distracted, or forgetful. But the most common cause of parched plants is watering them on a set timetable. "Do not put your plants on a watering schedule," warns houseplant specialist Vivian Mitchell of Merrifield Garden Center in Merrifield, Virginia. "Water only as plants request watering," she advises. Plants make their initial request for watering by drooping slightly.

Symptoms. A thirsty plant wilts and perks again when watered. The leaves of a chronically dry plant (one that gets some water, but not enough) will turn brown along the leaf margins and out to the tips. This is a sign that the dehydrated soil has accumulated too much salt and the plant tissue has burned. Older leaves will turn yellow and drop from the bottom of the stalk as their nourishment is sucked away to feed new growth. Note the contrast with overwatered plants, which turn black only at tip of the leaf and have generalized, not localized, yellowing.

Cures. Water the plant when it's dry about one third down from the top. And check with an expert to make sure this is exactly what each plant requires. Some plants need to be kept moist all the time and some like to dry out thoroughly between watering.

3. **Overpotting.** Just as you wouldn't buy a pair of shoes three sizes too big and wait to grow into them, you shouldn't put a small plant in an enormous container and expect it to grow into the pot. Your plant will be uncomfortable in its "big shoes"; it won't thrive and may even die. Plants prefer containers that allow them to extend their roots throughout, pulling in moisture and nutrients from every corner. When you attempt to keep the soil moist in a big pot with tiny roots, there is greater danger of rot because the water displaces the soil's oxygen, causing the root system to stagnate.

Cures. Keep a new plant in the container it comes in unless you see roots growing right out the drainage holes. When you do repot, choose a container that is only one or two sizes larger than the old one.

4. **Wrong soil.** The general rule is to use only professionally produced potting medium—never "dirt" from the garden or any other dense or heavy soil. When you purchase plants at a nursery or garden shop, they are planted in the right mixture. When you're repotting, use only soil marked "houseplant potting medium" for the job, and use fresh soil; never recycle soil from another plant.

5. **Wrong light.** You must know the requirements of your individual plants to get this one right. If the plant didn't come with instructions, look in a plant book or call a nursery and ask.

Symptoms. Flowering plants (African violets, cyclamen, poinsettias, cactus) usually need a high amount of light to bloom and won't flower without it. Plants that tolerate only low light will burn and develop an all over yellow-to-brown look if left in direct sun or in a very bright room. Nonflowering houseplants that get too little light may lose color and drop leaves; or they may become leggy as the plant stretches toward the light.

Cures. Those blue "plant-grow" light bulbs are fine to supplement inadequate daylight. But exclusive use of artificial incandescent bulbs will focus too much warmth on the plant. If you are really short of daylight, use a fluorescent bulb in combination with the plant bulbs. Don't expose any plants to light for more than twelve hours at a time. If a plant shows symptoms of too much light, move it!

Easy-to-Grow Vegetables and Flowers

There are two tricks to gardening well, and both are simple. First, choose plants that will thrive in your climate zone and with your soil type, sunlight, and rainfall patterns. Second, stick with easygoing flowers and vegetables. Here are a half dozen of each that will grow well in most any garden.

 FLOWERS

1. **Marigolds.** These golden frilled flowers are easy to grow from seed. They like hot, sunny weather and ask only that you pinch off the dead blooms to make room for new ones. They'll also pitch in and help with your vegetable garden by keeping pests away (see below).

2. **Snapdragons.** Tall, colorful, and graceful, snapdragons are beautiful *and* fun: squeeze their little "mouths" together and see the dragon snap. Plant them from seed or (for quicker blooms) plant seedlings. They like full sun and well-drained soil.

3. **Zinnias.** Talk about cooperative—the more you pick these brightly colored flowers the more they grow! Like marigolds, they are easy to cultivate from seed and like full sun and well-drained soil.

4. **Impatiens.** These small, pastel flowers will thrive in shady areas. A separate variety (New Guinea impatiens) has brightly colored blossoms and can be grown in full sun. Both kinds need plenty of water and wilt quickly on hot days. They do come back when watered, but don't count on their surviving many of these "near-death" experiences.

5. **Sunflowers.** These giant-headed flowers grow up to ten feet tall from little black seeds (the same ones

we snack on). Tie the stem to a large, sturdy stake to keep the massive flower head from falling over as it shoots toward the sky.

6. **Pansies.** Now here is an unfairly named plant. These jewel-toned, velvety flowers don't live up to their wimpy name. They are among the hardiest flowers you can grow. They can bloom from late summer straight through fall and into winter, long after other flowers have succumbed to the cold. Plant pansies from seedlings and pinch off the dead blooms to encourage new growth. If the plant gets leggy, cut the foliage back and the feisty little pansy will bounce right back.

 Vegetables

1. **Zucchini.** Zucchini grows so easily and so quickly that you may have a hard time keeping up with the harvest. Plant seeds following packet directions, planting each in a separate mound of earth. Allow at least a 5-foot circumference to accommodate the large and sprawling plant. Water, fertilize, and begin scouring your recipe books for new ways to cook zucchini!

2. **Tomatoes.** They come in many varieties, but the two easiest and most familiar are Early Girl (which can be harvested early, as the name suggests) and beefsteak, the huge meaty tomatoes so perfect for slicing and sprinkling with salt and olive oil. Plant tomato seedlings in the early warmth of spring where they will get full sun. Water them slowly and deeply during hot weather and fertilize regularly. You will need to stake the plant if it begins to topple. Pick tomatoes when all the green has been replaced by deep red.

3. **Onions.** Probably the easiest vegetable to cultivate, onions grow quickly when given sufficient water. You

can plant them from "sets" (small bulbs) or put the whole onion in the ground. For variety—and a fun project—plant some sets or onions about 8 inches deep and the rest about 3 inches beneath the surface. The deeply planted onions will elongate to reach the surface and grow up to be scallions; the more shallow plants will become round yellow onions!

4. **Green beans.** These mature quickly from seeds and produce abundant crops. Choose bush beans (there are several varieties) and seed a new batch every few weeks to keep up a steady harvest. Pick when the pods are about four inches long.

5. **Peppers.** Buy these plants as seedlings and consider a mixture of hot and sweet plants. If you plant a little cilantro, you'll have the ingredients for homemade salsa (tomatoes, onions, and peppers) right in your own garden.

6. **Lettuce.** If you want to plant something for cool-weather gardening, lettuce is a very satisfying choice. Plant from seeds, keep watered, and you'll be harvesting your salads within six weeks.

OUTSMARTING GARDEN PESTS To make life a little harder for the insects who'd enjoy snacking on your vegetables, avoid planting all of the same crop together. Mix up the seeds and seedlings so the rows have a smattering of each vegetable. Putting tomato next to squash, which is right beside corn, will thwart insect pests who like to munch their way straight down a row of all one kind. "Insects are pretty picky eaters," says Tom Christopher, coauthor of *The Twenty Minute Gardener;* "most of them have adapted to live on a certain plant—for example, tomato horn worms really only want to eat tomatoes." This technique works even better if you add herbs and other aromatic plants like marigolds to the mix. The strong scents make it harder for pests to recognize their favorite foods.

 # Basic Gardening Tools

When it comes to gardening tools, buy the best you can afford. A well-made tool will last longer, be kinder to plants, and make the job easier for you. Gardening experts advise checking the quality of the metalwork and paying attention to the way parts are joined together. The blade or metal head of the tool should be welded to a socket that fits up around the handle, not jammed directly into the handle where it will soon come loose. Avoid buying tools with painted wooden handles because the paint is there to disguise inferior wood (and it will also chip off on sweaty palms). Before you buy any tool, grab and use it as you would in the garden. Seize the trowel and twist your wrist as you might when scooping a planting hole, put your foot on the top of the spade as if you were digging, and so forth. This is the only way to find out if the tool is the right size for your height, your hand, and your strength.

1. **Pruner.** For cutting back flowers and plants and pruning deadwood and twigs. Buy the best you can afford because cheap ones don't cut cleanly and can damage branches, causing rot or disease over time.

2. **Trowel.** For digging out weeds and planting flowers and bulbs. You may want two: narrow for weeding and planting bulbs, and broad for flowers and seedlings.

3. **Spade.** A spade is one of the most important garden tools you'll buy. This long-handled tool is used for planting trees and shrubs, making trenches along garden beds (for drainage), and many other digging and earth-turning jobs.

4. **Knife.** A one-piece knife with a serrated blade and metal handle—a steak knife is perfect—may turn

out to be your favorite gardening tool. It will dig weeds with pinpoint accuracy and plunge through the soil neatly in narrow spaces. (Don't use a wooden-handled steak knife with a flexible blade because it won't be strong enough.)

5. **Leaf rake.** A bamboo rake is inexpensive and gentle on your grass and plants.

6. **Watering can.** Good-quality cans will come with a brass tip, called a rose. A good rose allows for precise and delicate watering.

7. **Gloves.** Some gardeners turn up their nose at gloves because they get between your hand and the soil. If you have sensitive skin, or value your fingernails, that's precisely the reason you might want to wear them.

8. **Straw hat.** It should go without saying (but it doesn't) that you don't want to be working in the garden for a couple of hours without protection from the heat and sun.

9. **Large plastic trash can.** Buy a light one so you can drag it around easily as you move through the garden digging weeds, pruning, and cutting away annuals. Plastic bags can blow away, and reopening them every time you throw something away is an annoying waste of time.

Social Life

7

It may seem incongruous to make checklists for having fun. But certain kinds of fun are a lot more enjoyable if you've planned adequately. Whether you are throwing a party, buying a gift, or expressing thanks for a service well done, a bit of thinking ahead will make your social life even more rewarding—and less worry will make it much more fun!

Tips for Throwing a Party

Details, details, details. Those are the three secrets for throwing a successful party. And creating checklists is the way to make sure you nail down every one of them! This list will help you focus on the most important details, and give you some suggestions for keeping track of them.

1. **Make a list,** suggests Suzanne Williamson, author of *Entertaining for Dummies,* and an experienced party planner and fellow list maker. Actually, make three:
   - A shopping list of everything you need to buy— don't forget cocktail napkins and smaller plates if you're having a dessert or cocktail party, or candles for a birthday cake!
   - A task list of all the things you can take care of before the day of the party.

- A Day of the Party list for everything that must be done on The Day.

2. **Make up the guest list** at least three weeks ahead of time.

3. **Send invitations** no later than two weeks before the party. The invitation, whether written or telephoned, should let your guests know whether dinner will be served at the party.

4. **Plan the menu** (or call the caterer) two weeks ahead of time. (Very popular caterers in large cities may need to be booked more than two weeks ahead.)

5. **Get help.** If you're expecting more than eight or ten people, give serious thought to hiring an extra pair of hands—a bartender or even a local teenager can take coats and bus the buffet table. If you do have a bartender or other assistant, explain exactly what you'd like him to do. Tell him where to find extra supplies and make sure he can direct guests to the bathroom and telephone.

6. **Assign tasks.** Decide who is going to make drinks and answer the front door. Consider hiring a bartender if you are the only host.

7. **Set the table.** If you're renting linens and tableware, reserve what you need at the rental store two weeks ahead. If you're buying disposable party ware, make this purchase well in advance to free yourself for other details.

8. **Stock the bar.** Buy drinks and mixers well ahead (see "The Well-Stocked Bar" on page 115 for what to buy). Don't forget to include nonalcoholic beverages.

9. **Decorate.** You don't need balloons or banners unless they are appropriate for the occasion. Flowers and candles, however, can add to the festive air and create a magical atmosphere. Place small vases of fresh flowers in several locations and scatter or

group candles where they'll glitter but be out of the way. Order flowers ahead of time, but don't pick them up until the day of the party.

10. **Round up extras.** Borrow any extra tables and chairs you need ahead of time so you can decide how to arrange them.

11. **Make sure you have plenty of hangers** and space to hang guests' coats. If you'll be tossing them on a bed, don't send guests to find the room on their own. Consider asking a neighbor's older child to handle this chore.

12. **Prepare the bathroom.** Don't forget fresh soap and clean hand towels for your guests. Cotton fingertip towels are a nice touch; but attractive paper towels are okay too. Make sure there's a wastebasket handy. Double-check the toilet paper supply.

13. **Strike up the band.** Give some thought to the mood you'd like to establish and select the CDs you intend to play a few days ahead of time. (A critical detail like this can get lost in the frenzy of last-minute preparations.) Unless you're hosting a dance party, keep the sound at a level that allows guests to chat comfortably.

14. **Keep a close eye on the food table.** Clear used glasses, plates, and crumpled napkins while the party is in full swing. Replenish food as needed. You might ask the coat taker to help with this job.

15. **Do your job.** Be a cheerful host. If tension or behind-the-scenes catastrophes have you longing for the end of the evening, your guests should never suspect it. No matter how frazzled, frustrated, or nervous you feel, keep smiling. Do your best to smooth their entry. Guests should have a drink in hand and be introduced to someone else within a few minutes of their arrival. It's your job to guide them to both bar and conversation.

☑ Rules of Thumb for Food and Drink

Keep these figures and tips in mind as you plan for any occasion.

1. **Drinks.** One 750 ml (fifth size) bottle of wine will serve six 4-ounce glasses. One 750 ml (fifth) of liquor will pour thirteen 2-ounce drinks. Most guests will average about three drinks each (or about a drink an hour). If you are serving only wine, allow about half a bottle per person.

2. **Ice.** One 5-pound bag of ice will fill about twenty 12-ounce glasses.

3. **Nibbles.** Guests will eat about four or five hors d'oeuvres in an hour and a half. For a three-hour party, with 30 people, you'll need 300 pieces. Plan to serve four or five different kinds of hors d'oeuvres at a cocktail party where food will be passed.

4. **Create food stations.** Make things a bit easier on yourself by placing attractive and tasty dips around the room. If your guests can help themselves to a platter of fresh vegetables or cheese board, you won't have to pass hors d'oeuvres every minute.

5. **Think variety.** Mix flavors, textures, and temperatures. If you have two cold dips in the room, for example, pass some hot hors d'oeuvres. If you're serving spicy salsa, offer some mild canapés too.

6. **Don't scrimp on shrimp.** If you are serving fresh shrimp with cocktail sauce, allow for at least six or eight shrimp per person—no matter how many other hors d'oeuvres you serve. Even the daintiest and most genteel of guests has been known to hover over the shrimp platter.

The Well-Stocked Bar

There's no foolproof way to stock a bar because there is no reliable way to predict what any guest might ask for. Even if you're not prepared to whip up a Pink Squirrel or Fuzzy Navel, you can still have a respectably well-stocked bar by stocking everything on this list. Purchasing everything at once will be an expensive investment, so you might start with the most frequently requested beverages and fill in from there. This list is arranged in order of popularity to help you plan your purchases. (See "Rules of Thumb for Food and Drink," above, for advice on quantities.)

1. **Hard liquor**
   - Vodka. Vodka accounts for one out of every four bottles of liquor consumed in the United States. It outsells Scotch, Canadian, and Irish whiskeys combined.
   - Scotch.
   - Gin.
   - Bourbon.
   - Rum (especially popular in the summer).
   - Vermouth (dry for mixing martinis, sweet over the rocks as an aperitif).
   - Tequila. Unless you're making margaritas, there isn't much call for tequila. (Tequila + Cointreau or triple sec + lime juice = margarita. You can also purchase margarita mixes at grocery or liquor stores.)

2. **Beer** remains the most popular alcoholic beverage in this country. Its sales easily eclipse those of all other "adult" beverages.
   - Premium domestic
   - Premium imported
   - Non-alcoholic

3. **Wines**
- White. Offer one or two crowd-pleasing varieties. Chardonnay is a white wine on the fruity side; Pinot Grigio is a drier white, and is gaining on Chardonnay in popularity.
- Red. Merlot is roughly the red-wine equivalent to Chardonnay, popular for parties or as a drink before dinner.
- Brandy.
- Champagne. You may not serve it at every party, but having a bottle or two on hand can make for memorable last-minute celebrations.

4. **Cordials and liqueurs** are either generic, such as sambuca, triple sec, and peppermint schnapps, or brands, such as Kahlúa, Grand Marnier, Drambuie, and Cointreau. If you intend to have a full-service bar, you'll want to stock whichever are necessary ingredients in your favorite mixed drinks. Cordials and liqueurs are, of course, also offered with (or after) coffee at dinner parties.

5. **Nonalcoholic beverages and mixers.**
- Juices. Tomato, cranberry, and orange juices are popular alone or as drink mixers.
- Bottled water. Offer both sparkling and still.
- Ginger ale.
- Tonic water and club soda.
- Coke or Pepsi.
- 7UP or other noncaffeinated soda.
- Diet soda.
- Iced tea or lemonade (for daytime parties).

6. **Condiments and drink accessories**
- Lemons and limes.
- Tabasco and Worcestershire sauces.
- Olives and cocktail onions.
- Rock salt (for margaritas).
- Bitters for making manhattans.
- Ice, bucket, and tongs.

Hosting Houseguests

Being a gracious host to houseguests is very different from entertaining people for a few hours on Saturday night. You and your guests will be in close proximity for at least a day or two; for the sake of your sanity and theirs, don't feel you must entertain them every minute of their stay. Your duty is to make guests feel at home. Offering some activities or amusements will help; over-booking them will not.

1. **Issue clear invitations.** Invite guests for a specific amount of time and mention a departure day. You'll save embarrassment and hurt feelings by tactfully letting your company know ahead of time when the "house party" will end.

2. **Help them pack.** Tell guests what activities you have in mind (boating, skiing, black-tie party, and so forth) so they can pack accordingly. If weather is an issue, advise them about the local forecast.

3. **Show them the ropes.** After guests arrive, tell them where to find what they need (towels, extra blankets, etc.) and how your household runs. (Is it okay to help themselves to the refrigerator? Is the cat allowed out?)

4. **Explain mealtime plans.** If you have specific plans for meals that include your guests, let them know ahead of time. If you expect guests to help themselves for certain meals, tell them what is available and where to find food and dishes. Better yet, set things out ahead of time.

5. **Don't overschedule guests.** Don't feel you must entertain guests all day and all evening long. Just as you'd probably like some quiet time to yourself,

your guests may, too. Ease into this with a clear sug-
gestion: "I thought you'd appreciate an hour to
yourself . . ."

6. **Pamper them.** A few special touches will make
them feel at home—only better.

Creating a Cozy Guest Room

When you're setting up a guest room, do it with the comfort and convenience of your guest in mind. If you are able to go beyond the basics, include a few extra touches to make your guests feel pampered. But even if you can't turn your guest room into the Ritz, spend a night there yourself to make sure all the amenities are in place. Your guest room should include:

1. **A comfortable bed.** Firm mattress, clean, soft sheets, two pillows per bed, one firm enough for reading in bed (or extras for that use), blanket, bed-spread and extra blankets, and a mattress cover.

2. **Box of tissues**—one for the bedroom, one in the bathroom.

3. **Reading light.**

4. **Water glass** or tumbler near the bed.

5. **Adequate closet and drawer space.** If draw-ers in the room are usually in use, clear a few be-fore guests arrive and point them out. Provide wooden or padded hangers for jackets and skirts or pants.

6. **Alarm clock.**

7. **Radio.**

8. **Wastebasket.** One in the bedroom, one in the bathroom.

9. **Bathroom amenities.** Soap and towels are re-quired; but toothpaste, shampoo, a hair dryer, and other toilet articles will be a welcome surprise.

10. **Telephone.** Not necessary, of course. But a nice touch if you have a spare jack.

11. **Reading material.** Provide a selection of current magazines and books, including short story collections.

12. **Fresh flowers.** A vase of flowers welcomes guests and suggests their visit was anticipated with pleasure.

How to Be a Great Guest

Being a good guest isn't all sipping cool drinks and lounging on the furniture. It takes a certain amount of care to do it right. Whether you've been invited for drinks, for dinner, or for the weekend, treat your hosts as thoughtfully as you hope to be treated by them.

DINNER AND OTHER PARTIES

1. **Learn some French.** RSVP stands for *respondez s'il vous plait.* Literally, it means "please respond," but the practical translation comes down to this: "Hey, tell me if you're coming or not, because I have food to buy and chairs to borrow!" If the invitation asks for your response by a certain date, call your host by then—he really does need to know. Only when an invitation says "regrets only" is it okay to say nothing and just show up.

2. **Forget "fashionably late."** Promptness is very chic—and the mark of a really great guest. If you're going to a dinner party, where timing can be critical for the host, it's rude, not fashionable, to arrive more than ten to fifteen minutes late. If the event is a cocktail or informal party, you can push the margin considerably more—to half or three quarters past the appointed hour. Never show up early.

3. **Don't be shy.** Even if you are a bit bashful, struggle out of your shell, if only as a kindness to your host. He's hoping guests will mingle and enjoy themselves. If you don't know anyone, start by asking the person next to you how she knows the host. This opening gambit often leads smoothly to other

topics and chances are you'll soon be chatting away. Don't spend an entire party talking exclusively to one person.

4. **Free the host.** Chat with the host and hostess, but don't monopolize them. Their mingling responsibilities are even heavier than yours!

5. **Be gentle.** Remember that you're a guest in someone else's home. This isn't the time to pound your fist on the table to make a point, to speak harshly to other guests, or, God forbid, to correct their children.

6. **Enjoy the food.** You don't have to stuff yourself, or ingest any foods you loathe or are allergic to. But there's no need to announce your vegetarianism at the start of a pig roast, or your aversion to fish as you arrive at a clambake. If you have severe allergies to common foods, tell your host ahead of time which foods could make you seriously ill. Otherwise, eat what you can and confine your discussion of the food to offering compliments to the cook.

7. **Greet the host.** If you've slipped into a large party unnoticed by a preoccupied host, find and greet him before you launch yourself into the festivities. By the same token, don't leave without seeking out your host or hostess to say good-bye and tell them how much you've enjoyed yourself.

8. **Give thanks.** Even if you've thanked them profusely the evening of the party, it's good manners to telephone the next day and thank your hosts for a good time. A handwritten note isn't required, but it's a gracious touch.

9. **Nix the flowers.** Not entirely, of course. But arriving at a party with flowers in hand can put extra pressure on a busy host. He'll have to put aside other pressing duties to find a vase, cut stems, and

arrange flowers. If you like, you could transport a bouquet already arranged in a vase. Otherwise, it's better to send flowers before or after the party.

10. **Watch for your cues.** Do this and you'll avoid faux pas (see page 130) and endear yourself to the host. Go in to dinner when the host announces it's ready (guests who worry about "going first" can drive a host crazy); wait for the host or hostess to lift a fork before you start eating, take "no" for an answer if your offer of assistance is declined; and notice when the host has stopped refilling glasses or introducing new topics of conversation. That's your cue to say "Thanks and good night."

WEEKENDS AND OVERNIGHT STAYS

Being a delightful houseguest is an art. In theory, you are an honored and pampered, albeit temporary, resident of the household. In practice, you are likely to be honored only if you don't expect to be pampered. A delightful houseguest does his level best to make no special demands. He is helpful or out of the way, talkative or quiet, and always game for anything—depending on the requirements of the moment. And he accomplishes this skillful feat while appearing to have the time of his life. But that's not all. A really great houseguest, the kind who is invited again and again:

1. **Arrives and departs on schedule** to avoid inconveniencing his hosts or putting them through the embarrassment of prompting him to depart.

2. **Keeps his room neat** and bed made, no matter what his habits are at home.

3. **Leaves the bathroom immaculate,** whether or not he shares it with other members of the household.

4. **Gamely pitches in** to help out with a variety of household chores—stirring the soup, changing a light bulb, wiping up a spill, taking out the trash, setting the table, and so forth.

5. **Resourcefully entertains himself** with a book, walk, nap, errand, or other independent activity to allow his hosts privacy and relaxation time during his visit.

6. **Hosts a meal.** Not only does he not expect home-cooked meals every night of his visit, he offers to take his hosts to dinner once or twice, depending on the length of his stay.

7. **Occupies himself** quietly if the hosts are asleep and he is wide awake.

8. **Removes the sheets** from his bed the day of his departure and remakes the bed with the spread. Stacks used sheets and towels neatly in his room.

9. **Thanks his hosts** with a thoughtfully chosen gift and gracious note.

Gift-Giving Tips

The secret to giving "the perfect gift" is threefold: Consider the occasion; think about what the recipient might need or want; and make sure the choice and cost are appropriate for the person and the occasion. Sometimes choosing a gift takes nothing more than common sense and a good idea. Occasionally, however, the process requires attention to the finer points of etiquette and a sharp eye for personal taste and habits.

1. **Don't give money to colleagues** or business associates. It could be misinterpreted as charity or—worse—a bribe.

2. **Plan your spending carefully.** Don't embarrass a friend or colleague with an unexpectedly lavish gift.

3. **Be careful when giving liquor.** A good bottle of wine is perfect for a connoisseur, tactless for a teetotaler.

4. **Get the holiday right.** Be sure the gift you send is for the holiday your recipient observes.

5. **Consider personal tastes.** If you don't know them, don't assume. Giving books or CDs without knowing something about the person's interests or tastes may seem presumptuous. Or it could look as if you chose in haste or desperation.

Tip Are you in a situation where you continue to exchange gifts with someone although your relationship has changed and the ritual has become meaningless? Etiquette maven Peggy Post advises, "be frank." Suggest just exchanging cards or say something like "Write us your family news—that will be the best present of all."

Stress-Free Holiday Giving

The only thing worse than racing through crowded stores buying too many gifts for an extended network of family, friends, and colleagues is to do it when you're frazzled, exhausted, and racing against the clock. What's that you say—this is your annual routine? Try these tips and see if the season doesn't get a little merrier.

1. **Shorten your list.** Buying fewer gifts will lower your holiday shopping stress level considerably. In a large family or office, suggest drawing names so each person buys a gift for just one other. Or consider buying gifts only for children in your extended families; easing the burden on the adults will be a gift in itself.

2. **Buy throughout the year.** When you see the perfect item, don't wait. If you don't buy it now, you risk finding it gone or forgetting about it when December rolls around. The more gifts you pick up before the season starts, the more you'll enjoy the season itself and the less you'll burden your wallet all at once.

3. **Buy when you're traveling.** Keep holiday giving in the back of your mind as you browse interesting shops on your next trip away from home. Shopping while traveling is often more fun and less stressful, and the people on your list will be pleased that you thought of them while you were away.

4. **One size may fit all.** Don't be afraid to give the same gift to several people on your list. For example, sending amaryllis bulbs to each of your cousins or presenting homemade holiday bread to each of your neighbors or coworkers is perfectly acceptable.

5. **Buy as many gifts as possible on-line and through catalogs.** Staying away from crowded shopping malls is one of the best ways to avoid holiday-related stress.

6. **Be creative.** If you've been in a rut, giving the same old socks, ties, nightgowns, and perfumes to friends and family, try something different. It will probably be a lot more fun for the recipient and will definitely be easier for you. Here are some ideas you can try without even leaving the house:

   • Food is almost always a welcome gift. Mail order catalogs offer a vast number of selections, from whole hams to dainty petits fours. You can delight any number of people on your list with a couple of toll-free phone calls. Or add a personal touch with a gift from your kitchen: a sampling of your homemade cookies presented in a pretty pottery bowl will make a beautiful gift.

   • Museum shops offer a wide variety of appealing gifts. A gift from your nearest museum will give an elegant taste of local flavor to someone across the country.

   • Think green. Flowers, plants, dried wreaths, and even holiday centerpieces are available from a variety of catalog houses.

   • Gift certificates for any catalog or department store can remove the worry about choosing "the wrong thing" and still seem more thoughtful and personal than cold cash.

   • Personal services. Surely there are those on your list who would be thrilled to be treated to a massage, pedicure, facial, or similar indulgence from a local spa.

   • The most personal gift of all—something almost anyone would be happy to receive from you—is your time. You might give a friend a "gift certificate" for an afternoon of baby-sitting or a week-night home-cooked meal; your sister a day helping organize her closets; or your dad a weekend painting the garage. Gifts like these are limited only by your imagination and the time you are able to spare—and you never have to set foot in a mall.

Foreign Phrases You Should Know

You don't have to leave home to encounter foreign words and phrases. In fact, your next-door neighbor might wave and shout *"Ciao!"* as he roars off in his convertible; perhaps the characters in the novel of manners you're reading are obsessed with appearing *comme il faut;* or a friend may welcome you by saying, *"mi casa es su casa."* These people are all native English speakers, they're simply using words from another tongue to express certain thoughts more colorfully or succinctly than it's possible to do in English. Here are some words and phrases you're likely to encounter—learn these now to avoid *faux pas* later!

1. **Bildungsroman** (German). A coming-of-age novel. *Catcher in the Rye,* by J. D. Salinger, is one example, *Great Expectations,* by Charles Dickens, is another.

2. **Bon mot** (French). Literally, *bon* means "good" and *mot* means "word." Together the phrase means "a witty remark." You wouldn't ask someone to put in a *bon mot* for you with your boss, but you might congratulate your boss on her *bon mot* at the last staff meeting—thereby putting in a good word for yourself!

3. **Comme il faut** (French). In keeping with the proper way of doing things. Telling your hostess that dinner was terrible is not *comme il faut.*

4. **Dernier cri** (French). The latest thing; an up-to-the-minute trend or fashion.

5. **De trop** (French). Too much—way too much—of something.

6. **Fait accompli** (French). Literally, "accomplished fact." A *fait accompli* is something already done and

finished, so there's no use objecting or trying to change it.

7. **Faux pas** (French). A social error. Wearing blue jeans to a black-tie event is definitely a *faux pas.*

8. **Je ne sais quoi** (French). Literally, "I don't know what." It refers to that "certain something," a quality that's hard to define.

9. **Mi casa es su casa** (Spanish). "My house is your house," meaning "make yourself at home."

10. **Pied-à-terre** (French). An apartment, usually in the city, which is kept for occasional use.

11. **Plus ça change** (French). These words are understood as shorthand for the complete phrase that ends with *"plus c'est la même chose."* "The more things change, the more they remain the same."

12. **Q.E.D.** (Latin). Q.E.D. is short for *quod erat demonstrandum,* meaning "which was to be shown." You'll occasionally encounter *Q.E.D.* in speech and writing as a not-so-subtle way of letting readers or listeners know that the person making the argument believes he has proven his point.

13. **Quid pro quo** (Latin). Literally, "something for something." An equal exchange, tit for tat. "The union finally agreed to a pay cut, but its leaders insisted on *quid pro quo,* so the company added dental insurance to the benefit package."

14. **Raison d'être** (French). Literally, "reason for being." Protecting animals is the *raison d'être* of the Humane Society of America.

15. **Roman à clef** (French). A fictionalized account of actual events and real people; *Primary Colors,* the best-selling novel about Bill Clinton's 1992 presidential campaign, is a contemporary *roman à clef.*

16. **Savoir faire** (French). Literally "to know how to do." If you have *savoir faire,* your manners are pol-

Foreign Phrases You Should Know — Page 131

ished; you're unlikely to do or say anything that isn't *comme il faut*. "Even more than his good looks and charm, it was Cary Grant's *savoir faire* that made him an irresistible leading man."

17. **Sine qua non** (Latin). An essential element of something. A trimmed tree is the *sine qua non* of Christmas.

18. **Tête-à-tête** (French). Literally, "head to head." A private conversation between two people.

19. **Vox populi** (Latin) "The voice of the people." The term refers to the prevailing sentiment or popular opinion. "During President Clinton's impeachment trial, the *vox populi* seemed to indicate that he should not be removed from office."

20. **Weltanschauung** (German). A philosophy of life, a way of viewing of the world, as in, "His *weltanschauung* doesn't allow for happy endings."

21. **Weltschmerz** (German). A romantic sadness or pessimism; weariness with the world. "His *weltanschauung* has given him *Weltschmerz.*"

22. **Zeitgeist** (German). Literally, the spirit of the time. The outlook and taste characteristic of a time or generation; "Will future historians name greed and selfishness as the *zeitgeist* of the baby boom generation?"

Tips on Tipping: Who, When, How Much

The etiquette of tipping can be tricky. Technically, a tip is extra money given to show appreciation for good service. In reality, restaurants and other services expect you to add 15 to 20 percent to your bill and many businesses pay their employees accordingly, expecting them to earn much of their income in tips. Acknowledging this economic reality, and bowing to long-standing custom, most people rarely withhold tips, even if service is below par.

Nothing distracts from the pleasure of good service as much as feeling unsure of whom to tip and how much to give. Keep this checklist in mind to relieve you of those uncertainties.

ENTERTAINMENT

Restaurants: Tip 15 to 20 percent of the pretax food bill to the server and 15 to 20 percent of the wine charge to the steward.

Bartenders: Leave a dollar per round for small parties and 15 to 20 percent of the tab for larger groups. The same applies for cocktail waitresses.

Coat checking: Fifty cents to one dollar per coat is fine. The more expensive the establishment (or the bigger the city), the higher the tip.

Ladies' room attendant: If the attendant provides service—including handing you a towel— tip twenty-five to fifty cents. If she assists you in any special way, tip one dollar. If the person sits in a chair and does nothing, feel free to leave without tipping.

TRAVELING

Concierge. A five-dollar tip is appropriate for an extra service such as a special effort to get you good seats at the theater or a table at a trendy, but booked, restaurant. You can offer the money after each service or leave it at the end of your stay.

Housekeeping. Usually no tip is required for a one-night stay. Depending on the service, leave one to two dollars per night, per person. The more expensive the hotel, the higher the tip.

Room service. A 15 percent tip is standard; but check your bill (or the bottom of the room service menu) to make sure the gratuity isn't already included before you add to it.

Bellhops. Tip a minimum of one dollar per bag. Tip five dollars if you have three to five bags. If the bellhop opens your room, one to two dollars is appropriate. A five-dollar tip is standard for running an errand.

Skycaps and porters. Tip one dollar per bag.

Cruises. The 15 percent rule usually applies here. Figure you'll distribute approximately 15 percent of the cost of the cruise among the service personnel. Some cruise lines provide tipping guidelines; if you're uncertain what to do, the ship's purser can help.

Vacation resorts. Tip one dollar for service at the pool or on the beach unless one dollar would be much less than 15 percent of your tab.

 PERSONAL SERVICES

Hairdressers. You're off the hook if the salon owner cuts your hair; owners are not tipped, no matter what service they provide. Otherwise, tip the hairdresser 15 to 20 percent and give the shampoo person a dollar or two, depending on the cost of the haircut. If your salon provides envelopes for tipping, you may put in a 20 percent tip and ask the hairdresser or salon manager to distribute the money.

Barber. Tip 15 percent of the bill, but leave a minimum of one dollar.

Manicurist, pedicurist, massage therapist. Give between 15 and 20 percent of the bill.

 ## HOME SERVICES

Service people, including window cleaners, painters, repair crews, chimney sweeps, and others. Tip between ten and twenty dollars, depending on the size of the job and the number of days they are at your house (unless they own the business). Don't tip plumbers or electricians unless they perform service beyond the call of duty.

Deliveries. For grocery delivery, tip one dollar a bag. For pizza delivery, tip one dollar per pizza. If you order a full takeout meal, tip the delivery person as you would a waiter: 15 percent.

Doormen and building superintendent. Tip from one to five dollars, depending on the special services they do for you. For example, if the superintendent responds promptly and cheerfully to your call for a late-night plumbing emergency, five dollars would be a nice gesture. When your doorman performs a small, courteous service (holding a package for you or helping you with your luggage, for example), you may wait and offer him a few dollars for several weeks of such services, rather than giving him money each time. Christmas tipping is the main event in these relationships. (See below.)

✓ SUGGESTIONS FOR HOLIDAY TIPPING

Holiday tipping is optional, of course. But if you receive courteous and reliable service from certain people year round, a gift certificate or cash bonus is a nice way to show your appreciation.

Hairdresser, manicurist, babysitter/nanny, housekeeper. For the most part, cash or a carefully chosen gift certificate is a good choice for someone with whom you have a direct relationship. Depending on the length of time you've done business, the cost of the service, and your own budget, you may want to tip from $20 to $100.

Delivery people. Twenty dollars is appropriate for your postal carrier, Fed Ex and UPS drivers, and any other regular (daily or weekly) deliveries.

Trash and recycling crew. Give $20 per person if you've received reliable and friendly service.

Newspaper carrier. Give or send $10 to $20 if the paper arrives daily and lands reasonably near the porch.

Doormen and superintendent. Holiday tips are more than a way to express appreciation: for some workers, seasonal tips amount to 10 to 15 percent of their annual income. The amount you give may vary according to your budget, the number of special services you've received over the year, and the relative luxury of the building. There's no "right" amount. A 1998 survey by the *New York Post* found that most New York City residents tip anywhere from $30 to $100. Of course, in posh apartment buildings, a holiday envelope can contain up to ten times more.

How to Pack a Picnic

Sure, going on a picnic requires considerably more effort than serving dinner at the kitchen table. But in the end, all that planning, wrapping, packing, and schlepping is wonderfully rewarding. Caterer Edith Stovel bases much of her business on picnics. She believes that even the most ordinary food is special at a picnic. "It becomes more magical because you're not just sitting down and having dinner," she says; "when you go outdoors, it becomes an occasion."

 PICNIC ESSENTIALS

1. **Ground cloth,** blanket, straw mat, or whatever you'd like to sit on
2. **Plates**
3. **Eating utensils**
4. **Drinking glasses or cups**
5. **Paper napkins**
6. **Paper towels**
7. **Plastic trash bag**
8. **Insect repellent**
9. **Your food!**

 ELEGANT OPTIONS

1. **Tablecloth**
2. **Corkscrew**
3. **Candles, matches, and hurricane lanterns** to protect the flame from the breeze
4. **Vase and flowers**

5. **Wine glasses**

6. **China**

7. **Silverware**

8. **Cloth napkins**

 ## Tips for Packing the Basket

1. **Be prepared.** Keep one picnic basket packed with essentials stored away at all times. When the picnicking impulse strikes, all you have to do is buy or make the food and head for the hills.

2. **Consider owning two picnic baskets.** Unless your picnic is for two and your meal is very simple, you'll probably find it difficult to pack everything you need into one picturesque basket. Dedicate one basket to nonfood items, and pack the food in the other. You may also want to have a cooler for drinks and cold food.

3. **Keep food safe.** This is the most important issue when packing a picnic. Chill cold foods thoroughly before packing, then put them in an insulated container. Heat liquids like soup until very hot, then pour into a thermos that's been rinsed with boiling water. Wrap other hot foods in heavy-duty aluminum foil and put them inside an insulated container or wrap in a heavy cloth. If you're bringing raw meat, poultry, or fish to grill outdoors, keep it cold until you're ready to cook. If these items are frozen when you pack them, don't allow them to defrost at room (or air) temperature because bacteria can form on the warm outer surface even though they may be cold or frozen inside.

4. **Handle with care.** Foods that will be transported in a picnic basket (or cooler) need more delicate handling than food destined only to be stored in

the refrigerator. Put sandwiches, fruits, and other "squashable" items in sturdy plastic storage containers, rather than simply wrapping or bagging them. Place any fragile items not stored in containers carefully near the top of your basket. Leave sufficient room in the basket so your delicious meal doesn't emerge bruised and mangled from the pressure of being jammed tightly inside. For fresher sandwiches, pack fillings and bread separately so tuna salad, sliced tomatoes, and other moist ingredients won't make the bread soggy.

THROW PICNICS INSTEAD OF COCKTAIL PARTIES Picnics are the perfect plan-ahead entertainment precisely because you must do all the work ahead of time. There's no running to answer the door, hang up coats, or mix drinks. Once you've spread the picnic blanket, the heavy work is done and you're free to relax with your guests.

Correspondence

8

In these hectic times our stationery use has dwindled. Few of us, for example, need engraved calling cards; and fewer still can devote leisurely hours to the custom of depositing those cards upon the silver trays of absent friends. Instead, we communicate both casually and quickly most of the time, using e-mail and telephone calls, and this fact of modern life has left many people insecure about the "niceties" of written communication. These lists tell you what you need to know to send mail the old-fashioned way—with finesse.

A Stationery Wardrobe: Paper for Every Occasion

We probably know better than to wear jeans when invited to high tea, but do we know enough not to write the gracious thank-you note on a memo pad? This checklist suggests the basic types of stationery to keep on hand and offers guidelines about when and how to use them.

1. **Informals.** Most stationers sell these small fold-over note cards (sometimes simply called "fold-overs") by the box in various colors and designs. But

don't be confused by the name. These so-called "informals" can actually be quite formal, depending on the style you choose. If you select white or cream paper, your "informals" will be appropriate for the most formal correspondence—including replies to formal invitations and letters of condolence. (See page 144 for tips on writing letters of condolence.) You may choose to have your name or initials engraved, embossed, or printed on the front page.

2. **Personal or household stationery.** The most versatile stationery for general use is "monarch," 7 ¼ by 10 ½ inches. This distinctive size can be used for personal or household business letters (see page 146 for writing an effective complaint letter), and for correspondence relating to your job or career. It may include your name and address at the top, with telephone, fax, and e-mail address printed below the address line. If you print only your address, the paper will be suitable for use by anyone in the household, including guests.

3. **Correspondence cards.** They are appropriate for writing anything from brief business notes to personal thank-you notes and can be used to send or reply to informal invitations. Frequently these cards have the writer's name or initials printed, embossed, or engraved at the top. These cards may be the single handiest piece of stationery you own. Correspondence cards come in two sizes: 6 ½ by 4 ¼ inches and the slightly more casual 5- by 3 ½-inch size.

4. **Various greeting cards.** Purchase a variety of these to keep on hand. When you can just reach into your desk drawer and pull out a birthday, congratulations, or get-well card, you're more likely to follow through on your impulse to send best wishes to a friend. Having a stash of cards will be a lifesaver

when you suddenly remember Aunt Millie is about to have a birthday.

5. **Gift enclosures.** You'll never again have to buy a greeting card to accompany a gift if you keep these small, personalized cards on hand. Gift enclosure cards are usually about 3 inches wide and about 2 ½ inches high and are white or cream colored, often with the monogram of the gift-giver. They are frequently sold as part of a stationery set.

6. **Lined envelopes.** Keep these business-sized envelopes (9 ½ by 4 ¼ inches) on hand for mailing checks.

7. **Return address stickers or address embosser.** These can make paying bills and writing other informal correspondence go much faster. Don't use stickers on formal correspondence.

SOME NOTES ON NOTES

- You don't need to acquire every type of stationery on the list above. Start with two types of paper, one for notes and one for letters. Make sure you have one kind that's appropriate for more formal occasions.

- Make sure your note card envelopes meet the U.S. postal regulation minimum size of 3½ by 5 inches.

- As a practical matter, everyday correspondence should include the return address in the upper left front corner of the envelope. The Postal Service will accept return addresses on the back flap (because this is the custom with formal invitations). But you will do the USPS and yourself a favor by putting the return address on the front for most of your mail.

- Thank-you notes, letters of condolence, formal invitations and their replies should always be handwritten, preferably in black or blue ink.

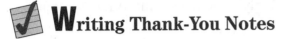

Writing Thank-You Notes

Writing a thank-you note may seem intimidating at first, but there's a kind of "formula" to writing them. A gracious thank-you note has characteristic traits; keeping them in mind will make the note much easier to write. Thank-you notes are:

1. **Prompt.** A note of thanks for an overnight stay should be written within a few days of your return home. Thanks for a wedding gift are within the bounds of courtesy if they arrive within three months of the wedding or of receipt of the gift, whichever is latest. (But if you want to keep from drowning in the task and be ultragracious, write each note shortly after the gift arrives.) Thanks for other gifts, such as birthday or holiday presents, should be sent within a week or two at the most. A note following a dinner party is optional, but if you do send one, write it within a week of the occasion.

2. **Sincere.** Focusing on sincerity will actually help you begin to write. Think about how you felt when you opened the gift and put that sentiment into simple words. Just a few sentences expressing these thoughts can constitute the entire note.

3. **Specific.** A note of thanks for "the lovely gift" sounds as if you've either forgotten what the gift was, or are writing the same generic note to everyone. Name the gift and say one thing about it—how you intend to use it, how beautiful it is, how nice of the giver to remember what you like, and so forth.

4. **Diplomatic.** Okay, so sometimes you receive a present that dismays you. Perhaps it is astonishingly ugly, or bizarrely inappropriate; these things do happen. It is, however, possible to write a sincere and

gracious note if you choose your words carefully and remember the old saying that it's the thought that counts. Here's an example. "Imagine my surprise when the carton of fresh bait arrived by express mail. It is certainly the most original gift I've ever received—and one I'll never forget. Thanks for making my birthday so memorable!" There, you've just thanked someone for sending you a box of worms—and there's not a sentence in the note that isn't true. Words and phrases like "interesting," "unique," or "never imagined I'd receive such an unusual gift" will be useful in diplomatic thank-you notes.

5. **Handwritten.** The essentially personal nature of a thank-you note requires that you write it with your own hand—not on a typewriter or computer. A handwritten note lets the recipient know that you care enough to put your personal touch into the effort.

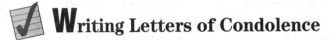 **W**riting Letters of Condolence

Writing to a friend or acquaintance who has lost a loved one can be a bit daunting. Nothing you say will lessen the grief, but a sincerely meant expression of sympathy can be an enormous comfort. And don't let fear of saying "the wrong thing" stop you from writing. Write the note as soon as possible after you hear news of the death, keeping these suggestions in mind.

1. **Write what you feel.** Stop and think about your reaction to news of the death. Many times this thought can be the first sentence of your note. A frank statement such as "We were shocked to hear . . ." or "I can hardly believe he's gone . . ." or "I never knew her, but news of your mother's death stunned me because I felt that I did . . ." lets the bereaved know you empathize with the loss.

2. **Speak of the dead.** If you knew the deceased, one of the best things you can do is recall a fond memory or mention a quality you admired or treasured in that person. Telling a friend, "Your father was so patient, I remember when he helped us build that tree house . . ." or "Aunt Gertrude was strict, but we always knew she had a soft heart . . ." will let the bereaved know their loved one will be cherished and remembered by others as well.

3. **Sympathize with the loss.** Even if you hardly knew, or never met, the deceased, your note can be a comfort. Let your friend or colleague know you are sympathetic to their grief. Simply saying "My thoughts are with you at this sad time" will do that.

4. **Don't assume you know how they feel.** Even if the deceased had been ill for a long time, don't refer to the death as "a blessing" or "a release" since

the person receiving your note might not feel this way. Instead, you might want to express admiration for grace and courage during a difficult ordeal. Never presume that an experience of your own qualifies you to say, "I know exactly how you feel." Such a statement may even anger or insult someone who is going through an intensely private emotional ordeal.

5. **It's okay to be brief.** You don't need to say much to convey your feelings of sadness and sympathy. And it's usually best to express yourself very simply: "Our hearts are aching to think of your grief at the loss of Joe." If you knew Joe, go ahead and say you'll miss him, too. Just a few sentences can say quite a bit.

6. **Don't leave it all to Hallmark.** There's nothing wrong with sending a sympathy card. But if you do, be sure to write at least one or two sentences in your own hand. Sending a commercially produced card with nothing but your signature at the bottom will convey a lack of feeling and may even be felt as an insult. A note written in blue or black ink on a white or ecru note card is the correct form for this occasion. (See page 139.)

7. **Avoid morbid details.** There is no need to mention details of a death. And it's especially important to avoid them if the circumstances were shocking or particularly unpleasant.

8. **Say only what you mean.** Sometimes we want to help, but feel inadequate because we have no idea what we could possibly do. Don't be embarrassed by the feeling, simply write, "I'd love to help in any way I can, please don't hesitate to call if you need anything." But include the offer only if you genuinely mean it; false sentiment will give your well-meant note a hollow ring.

✓ Writing Effective Complaint Letters

What do you do if your new car turns out to be a lemon? If the electrician installs the plugs and light switches on the wrong walls? Or if a clumsy waiter pours cranberry juice on your white dress? The first thing to do, of course, is discuss the issue with the manager of the business involved. But if you don't get satisfactory results at that point, don't give up: the next step is to write to the owner of the business or president of the company. Here are eight steps to guide you in writing an effective complaint letter.

1. **Name names.** Address your letter to a specific person. Sending a complaint "to whom it may concern" leaves you no way to affix responsibility and no one to call to follow up. Call the business's headquarters and ask for the name (and correct spelling) of the person in charge.

2. **Keep it simple.** Put in just enough detail, such as dates, locations, and names of personnel, to make your point clear. A multipage diatribe may overwhelm (or alienate) the person you're writing to. Your letter will have more punch and will be read more carefully if you explain the situation as briefly and clearly as you can.

3. **Hold your fire.** Forget about letting off steam. No matter how outraged you feel, you won't help your case by focusing on your anger or indignation. Use your letter to explain the problem and make a case for obtaining what you feel is owed.

4. **Name your price.** Well, not your price, really, but be sure you state clearly what you would like to have done about your complaint. Be specific: "I expect a full refund"; "I am counting on you to reim-

burse me for the $30 dry-cleaning bill"; "Please extend the warranty on my car for one year."

5. **Don't threaten.** This is not the time to threaten further action if your expectations are not met. Your letter should focus on what you believe is fair and reasonable and its tone should convey your expectation that the person you are writing to is a fair and reasonable person.

6. **Send Exhibit A.** If you have receipts, or other backup documentation for your complaint, enclose a copy (not the original) with your letter.

7. **Make a copy.** For your own reference, and just in case you do wind up pursuing the matter further, keep a copy of the letter for your file. It's a good idea to clip together your complaint letter, your receipts, and any other correspondence or notes from telephone calls.

8. **Follow up.** Another letter or a follow-up phone call is appropriate before you pursue further action. If you get as far as small claims court (see page 220) you'll be one step ahead.

Dealing with Death

If we're lucky, most of us have little firsthand experience dealing with death. The American Association of Retired Persons estimates that we lose someone close to us only about once every fourteen years. But our inexperience puts us at a disadvantage confronting the bewildering and costly array of decisions to be made at a time of such profound loss. Giving some thought in advance to handling a death can make a difficult time a bit easier.

✓ **W**hat to Do When Someone Dies

1. **Don't move the body** unless you have medical permission or a permit to do so.

2. **If the death was expected,** you may call the attending physician or a hospice nurse to sign the death certificate. (A death certificate is always required and must be signed by the proper authority.)

3. **If the death was unexpected** or its cause was uncertain, violent, unusual, or due to a contagious disease, dial 911 or call the police.

4. **Call a close friend or family member** to come and help you. Emotional support and an extra pair of hands can make a big difference.

5. **Ask whether the deceased had already made final arrangements** or had expressed wishes about what he or she wanted. Check to see if any prepayments have been made for funeral expenses and whether or not a burial plot has been designated.

6. **Determine whether and when there will be a funeral,** prompt burial, or a cremation and select the funeral home or crematorium that will take care of the arrangements. Depending on the weather, a body can be left at home (as is) for as long as seventy-two hours. So don't feel you must make a snap decision about where to send the remains if someone dies and no plans have been made.

7. **If you need to relocate the body** before burial plans are finalized, you can have the body picked up from a home or hospital and transferred to a funeral home for temporary storage, for which you pay only a transfer fee. Make sure this situation is understood by the funeral director so there is no mistake about your option to choose a different funeral home after you decide what you want to do.

8. **Inform friends and family** about the service once details have been finalized, or choose someone to do this for you. (See "Ten Facts You Should Know About the Death Care Business," below.)

9. **Keep careful track of the original death certificate** and make several extra copies. The death certificate will be essential when dealing with Social Security and insurance companies, and when selling real estate or other personal property that belonged to the deceased.

10. **If you don't already know,** ask someone close
    to the deceased where the obituary should appear.
    Consider alumni and trade magazines as well as
    newsletters for clubs and other special interest orga-
    nizations. The funeral home generally places an
    obituary in the local paper for a small charge.

Ten Facts You Should Know About the Death Care Business

1. **The average cost of a funeral** in the United States is $5,000—not including cemetery expense, which can add another $2,000 to $4,000. A funeral is the third-largest purchase, after a house and a car, for many American families.

2. **Every funeral home has a nondeclinable charge** called "General Services," which includes paperwork, overhead, preparing the body, use of the funeral home for visitations, memorial services, etc. Ask to have all charges broken out so you can comparison shop. General services costs can vary as much as 300 percent at funeral homes within one town or city.

3. **Be sure to compare bottom-line prices** among funeral homes. Some may charge more for general services, but less for coffins, urns, or other items that can make their total lower overall.

4. **Prices are regulated** by the federal Funeral Rule of 1984, which also requires funeral homes to make price lists available and quote costs over the telephone. This federal rule prevents funeral homes from charging any extra fees or making negative or intimidating remarks to you if you purchase a casket from another source. You may have a legitimate complaint for the Federal Trade Commission (FTC) if a funeral director refuses to cooperate.

5. **The casket is the most expensive item in a funeral.** A low-to-medium-priced coffin will cost about $1,700. But there are much less expensive choices, including canvas or cloth "pouches," which can be used for burial and even for viewing if you choose. If price is an issue, keep asking to hear your

options until you're satisfied you know what would be the least expensive. (Be prepared for a response along the lines of "Oh, you couldn't possibly want *this* for your loved one!" Don't be intimidated.)

6. **The cost of an urn can range** from less than $200 to as much as several thousand dollars for objets d'art that can be displayed at home. But the cremation fee includes a heavy cardboard or plastic container which you may keep as the final receptacle. Occasionally these will be stamped "For Temporary Use," but don't be fooled; they can be used for burial or for keeping ashes at home. Remember, you can always put the original container into a receptacle of your choice if you plan to keep it at home.

7. **If you're going to put the ashes in a mausoleum,** the owner may insist on your purchasing an urn to exempt his business from paying for another container if the original becomes damaged after several years.

8. **Caskets and urns can usually be purchased less expensively** from third parties than from funeral home. Many good casket deals can be found on-line, and often, caskets can be shipped overnight. See the Resources Section for Web addresses.

9. **No law requires embalming.** This is optional and strictly up to the family.

10. **Consumer groups advocate** researching and choosing burial arrangements before they are needed. But they strongly advise against the "preneed" payment deals urged by many in the industry.

Children
(For Those Who
Only Borrow
Them!)

If your children have long since left home, or if you entertain other people's children infrequently, you may find yourself at a loss when they come to visit. The lists in this section are aimed at helping you keep them safe, entertain them, and maintain your own sanity while enjoying their company.

✓ Childproofing Your Home

It's easy to miss potential child-safety hazards around the house. In fact, accidents are the number one killer of children—more than all childhood diseases combined—according to the National Safety Council. The good news is that home accidents are entirely preventable. One of the best ways to spot trouble is to literally crawl around the house, exploring it as a toddler might. This checklist will help you recognize and correct safety risks.

1. **Cover open electrical outlets** with plastic safety caps.

2. **Tie electrical cords together** and tape them down to prevent tripping.

3. **Keep shade and blind cords out of reach** or invest in the type that break apart if a child's head or limbs become entangled.

4. **Install childproof latches on cabinet doors** (for brief visits, use rubber bands or twine to keep handles closed).

5. **Lock away all household cleaners** and other toxic substances.

6. **Put safety gates or other sturdy blockades** at the top and bottom of staircases.

7. **Double-check windows and screens** to make sure they're locked.

8. **Protect little heads from sharp-edged furniture.** Cover any child-high tables with padding (try a mattress pad secured with duct tape) or purchase specially designed corner protectors. The type that attach with double-sided tape are, unfortunately, easy (and fun) for many toddlers to remove. Devices that fit around table edges like garters will be easier for you and safer for the child.

9. **Be on the lookout for top-heavy items** like bookcases, étagères, or other furniture that could be toppled or shaken, causing heavy objects to fall.

10. **Decks and balconies should be kept off limits** to unsupervised children. Tiny bodies can squirm through small spaces in railings.

11. **Check bathrooms for tempting but toxic items** like strawberry shampoos or vanilla-scented candles.

12. **Remove candy dishes** with nuts, small candies, and other choking hazards. Put away small items that children might swallow (buttons, small collectibles, pet toys, etc.).

13. **Store plastic dry-cleaning bags out of reach.**

14. **If you have firearms in the house,** make sure they're unloaded and out of reach. Store the ammunition separately.

Baby Gifts They'll Drool Over

Anyone reasonably well acquainted with a newborn has learned this hard truth: the world of babies is vast and bewildering for the uninitiated. Perhaps no one understands this better than a relative, godparent, or friend in search of the perfect baby gift. Ari Lipper, coauthor with his wife Joanna of *Baby Stuff: A No-Nonsense Shopping Guide for Every Parent's Lifestyle,* offers these suggestions:

1. **Ask if parents have registered for gifts.** Having a baby is right up there with getting married when it comes to receiving gifts—but new parents have less time to return what they don't need. Like newlyweds, many parents now register for baby items they would like to receive. Don't guess what to buy if the answer is as close as your nearest Toys 'Я' Us.

2. **Consider the unnecessary.** Think about items parents might like to have, but may not purchase because they're too busy buying necessities like cribs and diaper pails. The Lippers divide baby stuff into three categories: 1) Must have; 2) Might want; 3) Totally optional. Consider narrowing your gift list to categories 2 and 3.

3. **Think strategically.** If you'd like to give a present that isn't a duplicate destined for return, stay away from the most frequently chosen gifts: mobiles, infant carriers, infant seats, front carriers, monitors, bouncer seats, activity gyms, and black-and-white mirrors and toys. And unless you find one you just can't resist, stay away from stuffed animals; the crib will be crowded enough.

4. **Consider a deluxe version.** Even if the parents of your tiny pal are inundated with front carriers or diaper bags, you can still make a hit by giving the deluxe version of these items. Also consider luxury clothing like embroidered booties or a cashmere hat and sweater set.

5. **Think keepsakes.** Silver picture frames or baby cups, spoons or porringers engraved with the child's name or initials will delight parents and be cherished keepsakes throughout the child's life.

6. **Watch clothing sizes.** Size labels may be little help when you're trying to decide which teensy outfit to buy. "They can be erratic to say the least," says Lipper; "babies' bodies vary so much and grow so fast that clothing sizes can't be as precise as for adults." Very often, baby sizes run so small that a six-month outfit given to a five-month-old will be too snug. And be careful with clothing labeled "newborn": many babies outgrow these outfits before even before they make their appearance!

7. **Match size with season.** As you cleverly shop for clothes that will fit Baby several months from now, think about the season that will coincide with the size. If you're not careful, you could wind up giving an adorable snowsuit that will fit perfectly next summer.

8. **Shop catalogs.** If you're looking for creative ideas, are short of shopping time, or just prefer the convenience of catalog shopping, you're in luck. It's possible to purchase everything from stuffed animals and educational toys to strollers and safety items from the variety of catalogs available. See the Resources section for a few to get you started.

9. **Be practical.** Avoid baby clothes that are too delicate to withstand repeated washings and stay away

from clothes that appear confining or feel rough or scratchy. Don't buy bottles, cups, or other items in gimmicky shapes that make them hard to clean and invite bacteria growth.

10. **Check for safety.** To remove any doubt about a product you're considering, call one of these automated, toll-free hotlines operated by the U.S. government. For child safety seats, call the National Highway Traffic Safety Administration at 800-424-9393. To find out about recalls on other baby products, call the Consumer Product Safety Commission at 800-638-2772.

Ten Ways to Entertain Kids on a Rainy Day

It's bad enough when *you're* stuck inside on a rainy day—imagine how frustrating and disappointing it is for a child held prisoner by the weather. You can make the day a lot more fun for everyone with a little ingenuity and only a few simple props. Try some of these games the next time you find yourself hosting a bored and restless child (or two). And after they're all worn out, remind them that rainy days were made for curling up with a good book.

1. **Build something small.** Construct a tiny hut, fence, or other simple structure using glue and toothpicks.

2. **Play with their ears.** Have a game of "Seek the Sound." While children are out of the room, hide a clock, kitchen timer, portable radio, or any object that makes a steady and fairly loud noise. When they return, give them a certain amount of time to locate the sound.

3. **Bake or cook something.** Choose something easy to make and fun to eat. Simple cookies and candies are rewarding because you can let all but the very youngest children make a contribution to the cooking. "Spider candy" is lots of fun and easy to make: Melt a 12-ounce bag of semisweet chocolate chips in the microwave, stir in 6 to 8 ounces of crispy chop suey noodles, and drop by the spoonful onto wax paper. They are ready to eat when cool and firm. Yum!

4. **Dress up.** Get out old clothes, hats, scarves, and jewelry and help kids create costumes. Don't limit yourself to regular "dress up"—try making a super-

hero cape using a scarf and two safety pins or a pirate hat from newspaper.

5. **Make faces.** Let children use old makeup to change their faces. They can become anything from models to monsters with the right application of rouge, eye pencils, lipstick, etc.

6. **Play simple games.** Play good old rainy day pencil and paper games: hangman, tic tac toe, or even an impromptu game of "pictionary."

7. **Practice the arts.** Help them create art and jewelry with pasta. Mix a few drops of food coloring with a little water and a splash of rubbing alcohol. Stir in dried pasta and spread on newspapers to dry (the alcohol will help them dry within a few minutes). String pasta for chains or necklaces or paste different shapes and colors on paper to create mosaics.

8. **Get wet.** Let kids climb in the tub in bathing suits or washable old clothing and give them free reign with a set of watercolor paints. They can paint the tub, the tile walls, their bodies—whatever they like. When they've had enough, turn on the shower to wash it all down the drain.

9. **Put them through training.** Give them an "Outward Bound" experience by having them navigate an indoor obstacle course. The adventures should vary according to the children's age and skill level, but can include a crawl through a large cardboard box, a climb over a mound of throw pillows, a step-up-step-down challenge with a stool or large book, and a ball-toss (into a hat, basket, box, etc.).

10. **Have a parade.** Get out pots, pans, plastic bowls, and wooden utensils and be a marching band.

What to Leave for a Baby-sitter

When you leave children with a baby-sitter, you want to know the sitter is well prepared to deal with any situation that might come up. Assembling information ahead of time will add to your peace of mind and guard against the possibility that you might forget something important in the chaotic dash for the door. Label the list clearly and post it prominently so the sitter can't miss it, even if you forget to point it out. (See page 00 for important numbers to keep by your phone.)

 WRITE THESE DOWN BEFORE LEAVING THE HOUSE

1. **Phone number where you can be reached.**

2. **Time you expect to return.**

3. **Itinerary** of where you'll be and when, if appropriate.

4. **Phone number of a close neighbor.** Call your neighbor first to see if they'll be home and available if needed.

 SHOW SITTER WHERE THESE CAN BE FOUND

1. **Cell phone and/or beeper number.**

2. **Information about security system.**

3. **House keys.**

4. **Car keys.**

5. **Instructions for answering the telephone;** pad and pen for taking messages.

6. **Pediatrician's phone number.**

7. **Poison control center phone number.**

8. **First aid kit,** flashlights, fire extinguisher.

9. **Operating instructions for indoor and outdoor lighting.**

10. **Medication.** Include information on dosage and instructions for administering.

11. **Allergy list.** Include information on medication, if relevant.

12. **Cash for incidentals,** if necessary.

Moving

11

Many psychologists rank *moving* just after death, divorce, and the loss of a job as among life's most stressful events. There's no denying the trauma involved in saying good-bye to friends and familiar sights. But the stress of organizing a move can be lessened considerably by making a series of lists and taking care of details one at a time.

Choosing a Realtor

You will have a relatively personal relationship with the realtor you choose to help you buy or sell your home. If you're buying, you'll spend hours together driving through neighborhoods, you'll be talking about some of your hopes and plans for the future, and you may be disclosing certain financial details to this person. If you're selling, the realtor will be evaluating your home, suggesting improvements to help sell it, and giving an opinion on what it may be worth. So find someone you trust and who you feel understands your interests. You can scout for realtors by dropping by open houses. If you would like to talk further with a realtor you meet, ask for a card.

QUESTIONS TO ASK WHEN YOU'RE BUYING A HOME

1. **Are you a full-time or part-time realtor? Do you have other full- or part-time employment?** It's not impossible to do a competent job selling real estate part-time, but it's a whole lot more difficult. If you wanted to look at homes in the middle of the day, would this realtor be free to show them? Would this realtor be able to research neighborhoods as effectively as a full-time realtor who depends completely on real estate for income?

2. **May I have the names of three or four home buyers you've worked with recently and may I speak with them?** A "no" answer to this question should end the interview. Also, be wary if the realtor can't produce *at least* five names of people who have bought homes within the past twelve months.

3. **How well do you know the neighborhoods that interest me and how much do you work in them?** A realtor who is familiar with the areas you prefer will have a much better sense of prices and values and will know whether they are headed up or down. There is also a much better chance that you'll get an early crack at houses just coming on the market.

4. **Given what you know about my preferences, are there other neighborhoods you'd recommend I consider?** Suggestions of neighborhoods that are far from what you had in mind may be a sign that the realtor doesn't understand your needs. If the realtor has good ideas for you, all the better.

5. **Do you use the computer to help find homes?** Any agent who isn't accessing the Multiple

Listing Service (MLS) on-line is not keeping up with the latest information.

6. **Do you insist on a buyer/broker contract?** A buyer/broker contract is between you (the buyer) and the realtor (the broker). It obligates you to pay the realtor's standard commission, whether or not the realtor helps you find the house you eventually purchase. If you do sign a contract, ask the realtor ahead of time if she'll be willing to negotiate her commission fee if you choose a home that's being sold directly by an owner. (In a "fisbo"—for sale by owner—deal, the owner avoids paying a seller's commission. But he may be willing to help pay your realtor's buyer fee if it helps cement the deal.) If you do sign a broker's contract, make sure it's not for longer than thirty days.

Tip Whether you are a potential buyer or seller, drive around the neighborhood and jot down the names of realtors with "sold" signs. Don't be taken in by a large number of "for sale" signs under one realtor's name; some realtors will take listings at very high prices just to have their signs up. You are looking for realtors who actually sell homes. When you've collected some names, be sure to interview only the individual realtor whose name was on the signs—not just anyone at that real estate office.

 ## QUESTIONS TO ASK WHEN YOU'RE SELLING YOUR HOME

1. **How familiar are you with my neighborhood? What area(s) or neighborhoods do you usually work in?** Someone who personally knows the reputation of the schools, the neighborhood amenities, the crime rate, and so forth may be able to sell your home more convincingly than a realtor who looked up these statistics at the library.

2. **Can you give me a list of all the homes you've sold in the last year?** If there's any hesitation in complying with your request, look for someone else. Check the neighborhoods, price ranges, and number of sales on the list. Do they suggest experience with your type of home?

3. **May I contact any of these people as references?** Don't consider a realtor who balks at having you talk with past clients.

4. **What is the range and average price of the homes you've sold over the past three years?** You'll do better with a realtor whose bread-and-butter sales are in the same price range as your home and who has experience selling to the kind of buyers you are likely to find for your home.

5. **Will you draw up a detailed marketing plan for my house and put it in writing?** You're not looking to critique the plans as much as you are trying to determine what kind of commitment the realty company is prepared to make toward selling your house.

6. **How much money will you and your office spend marketing my home and can you put that figure in writing?** A real estate office that puts its marketing budget for your home in writing will very likely stick to it. This information also allows you to compare one realty company with another.

7. **Will you have a flyer box in front of my house and will you keep it full?** Having flyers with the features your home offers is one of the best ways to get people interested enough to come see it.

8. **Do you plan to hold open houses? How many, how often?** Open houses are an effective way to expose your home to a large number of

prospective buyers. See the list below for getting the most out of them.

9. **What other advertising will you do to market my house?** The answer to this question is, of course, closely linked to the marketing budget. There are a number of ways to get your home out there where prospective buyers are likely to see it, and they cost money. On-site flyers with a sketch, photo, or floor plan of your home, and advertising layouts in newspapers and real estate magazines, are just a few possibilities to ask about.

10. **Are you experienced working with buyers who might be good prospects but don't necessarily have a 20 percent down payment or perfect credit?** When buyers have trouble coming up with money, the realtor who can point them toward creative financial solutions has an enormous edge over one who can't. It's an even bigger plus if your realtor has connections with agencies or financial institutions that are ready to assist potential buyers.

Preparing Your Home for Sale

From a buyer's point of view, the most appealing homes are those that look as if they could be moved into right away. The more your home gives this impression, the faster it is likely to sell. One of the most effective techniques for making your home appealing is to keep the interior pleasant, but neutral. "Most buyers have very little imagination," according to top-selling realtor Barbara Shoag, "so if the house is cluttered or has dramatic wallpaper, most people will be put off because they can't see past the highly personal decorations."

1. **Repair anything broken:** loose boards, dangling fixtures, cracked windows, etc.

2. **Take a look at your house from the outside.** Does the trim need painting? Does the exterior paint look dreary?

3. **Fix chipped paint or peeling wallpaper.** Paint a neutral color inside.

4. **If you are planning to replace your carpet,** choose a neutral color (gray or beige).

5. **Tidy each room** and arrange each one as invitingly as possible.

6. **Put away** any highly personal or eccentric decorative items.

7. **Plant colorful flowers** or put attractive flower pots or window boxes in front of the house to add to your home's curb appeal.

HOLDING A SUCCESSFUL OPEN HOUSE Think of your open house as an opportunity to show prospective buyers what a gracious home and comfortable life they would enjoy if they bought your place, and set the stage a little bit to get their imaginations going.

Clean the house, of course, and pick up any clutter. Set the dinner table attractively and place vases of fresh flowers in various rooms. Turn on soft or classical music to create a relaxing mood. An hour or so before the open house, bake cookies or put something aromatic in the oven to give the house an inviting smell. But avoid heavy air fresheners or other strong artificial scents. Turn on all the lights in every room no matter what time of day it is. And finally, excuse yourself while the house is shown. Expert realtors find that if owners are around, potential buyers will say nice things and leave. If owners are away, buyers can express their concerns freely and the realtors can then discuss them in a candid way.

Choosing a House or Apartment

There's more to finding a place to live than falling in love with a cozy kitchen or big backyard. Scrutinize potential houses or apartments inside and outside before allowing the romance to carry you away.

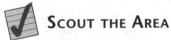

Scout the Area

1. **Pay attention to location.** Realtors aren't kidding when they say that the three most important points about any home are location, location, and location. Different people will have different preferences regarding location, but everything about the location of a house or apartment will affect your quality of life. Give careful thought to the town, the neighborhood, the street, and the building's location.

2. **Case the neighborhood.** Walk a few blocks in each direction to get a feel for the neighborhood. Are homes and yards well maintained? Beware if you see several "for sale" signs, which could indicate current or budding problems. Are businesses or industrial complexes mixed with residential areas? If so, are they likely to cause noise, traffic problems, unpleasant odors?

3. **Visit at night.** Go after dark, using the method of transportation you'll use when you live there. Do you feel safe in the train station at night? Is this an area where you'd feel comfortable walking after dark? Is it peaceful, or are vehicles, businesses, or residents making a lot of noise?

4. **Explore the "errand circuit."** Visit the nearest grocery store: Is it conveniently located? Would you

want to shop there? Are dry cleaner, drugstore, bank, post office, library, and other stops on your errand route easy to get to and pleasant to use?

5. **Look for lifestyle amenities.** How convenient are parks, theaters, places of worship, good restaurants?

6. **Talk to neighbors.** Don't be shy—if you move to the neighborhood, you'll want to talk to them occasionally anyway. Tactfully ask them to tell you the things they like most and least about living there. Residents are usually happy to chat with their prospective neighbors. If you encounter unfriendliness, take note.

7. **Check out local regulations.** If you're buying a home, quiz your realtor on zoning ordinances, property taxes, upcoming assessments, homeowner association rules, and other issues that will affect expenses on and control of the property. Your realtor can and should investigate these issues for you. If you don't get complete answers, go to city hall and track them down on your own.

 CASE THE JOINT

If you're purchasing a home, hire a home inspection expert to look the place over carefully and give you a report on his findings. If you're renting, you are generally on your own for checking out the soundness and quality of the building. Before you sign a lease, be sure to go over the items on this checklist.

1. **Look into utility costs.** If you're purchasing, ask to see utility bills for the past twelve months. If you're renting, ask about typical utility costs in each season, especially summer and winter.

2. **Turn everything on.** If refrigerator, stove, washer, dryer, or other appliances come with the place, make sure they work. Run the garbage disposal, turn on the stove, look at the temperature reading in the refrigerator and freezer. Turn on the heater and air conditioner. Note how long it takes each room to heat up or cool down.

3. **Test the water pressure.** Flush the toilet(s) while the shower is running and check the pressure and temperature in the shower. Run the kitchen faucet while another tap is open or flush the toilet while the water's running in the sink.

4. **Examine doors and windows.** Do they open easily and close securely? Are the locks in good working order? Do the windows have screens?

5. **Look closely at walls, floors, and baseboards.** Look for mildew or water stains on walls, ceilings, carpets, and floors. Pay close attention to warped boards or mottled, uneven walls; these could be signs of leaking pipes, roof, or general dampness. Use your nose to check for mildew as you open closets and cupboards.

6. **Keep an eye out for pests.** Carefully inspect corners and cupboards for droppings or other telltale signs of rodents or bugs. And, of course, traps are a dead giveaway.

 # Choosing a Mover

If you plan to use a professional mover, starting looking for one six to eight weeks in advance. Here are some tips to help you select a reliable mover and save money at the same time.

1. **Get three written estimates.** Call three companies and have their agents come to your home to prepare an estimate. Get enough detail from each company about what is included to be sure you're comparing like services. For example, do they charge extra for bulky items, elevators, or flights of stairs? How do their coverages for loss and damage compare? This will also protect you from discovering on moving day that services you thought were included actually cost extra.

2. **Ask three questions.** As you call around to movers, your first three questions should be: Do you send an agent out to do a free estimate? Are you licensed and bonded? Do you pay worker's compensation? Ask for a photocopy of the license and bonding paperwork.

3. **Understand the terms of the estimates.** Most moving companies will offer either a binding estimate (fixed price) or an estimate with a cap, which means you might pay less than that amount but won't pay more. Get the estimate in writing and think twice before agreeing to a nonbinding or hourly estimate without a cap.

4. **Don't pay for more mover than you need.** If your move is local or within your state, don't feel you must pay for higher-priced national movers to get quality service. Some movers specialize in smaller loads and local destinations and can charge

less because they avoid interstate commerce
charges.

5. **Check credentials.** Interstate movers are regulated by the Federal Highway Administration. Call
FHWA at 202-358-7106 to find out if your mover is
registered and insured (see the "Resources" section
for alternate phone numbers). Local movers may or
may not be regulated by your state. Check the government pages in your local phone book for an
agency to call.

6. **Get professional help.** Before you sign anything,
look for the words "agent labor only." This means
that the company uses only trained movers and
doesn't entrust your belongings to casual laborers
they don't know.

7. **Time your move for savings.** Summer is the
busiest time for movers, while November through
April tends to be very slow. Also, Saturdays and the
end of the month are generally the busiest times in
any season. If your schedule permits, you may save
10 to 15 percent by taking advantage of the slow
season. Don't be afraid to bargain.

8. **Pack yourself and save.** You can trim moving
costs considerably by doing the packing yourself.
On local moves, packing charges can make up as
much as half the fee. The company, however, will
not be liable for anything its workers did not pack.

9. **Investigate insurance options.** Most movers
offer very limited liability coverage unless you opt
to pay more. Before you do this, check with your insurance company. Your homeowner's or renter's policy may protect your goods during a move.

10. **Cheapest may not be best.** A low price may be a
sign that the mover will be cutting corners with
shoddy equipment or slipshod practices. Beware of

nonbinding estimates that look good up front, but turn into head-slappers at your destination.

11. **Handle with care.** No matter how reliable the mover, or how much insurance you've purchased, it's best to handle irreplaceable items (heirlooms, treasured jewelry, important documents) on your own.

Tip Each moving company that sends a representative to your home should give you a copy of "Your Rights and Responsibilities When You Move." This booklet is prepared by The Federal Highway Administration (FHWA) to guide you through the unfamiliar terrain of household goods carriers. It describes technicalities and defines specific terms like tariff, bill of lading, binding estimate, and flight charge. You may not think of it as exciting reading, but paying close attention to this publication can save you hundreds of dollars and much unwanted excitement in the course of your move.

Countdown to Moving Day

Moving an entire household from one place to another can seem overwhelming. How will you get it all done, or even keep track of everything that must be done? With this countdown checklist, you'll have the security of knowing exactly what you must do *and* the pleasure of ticking off each item as you accomplish it.

TWO MONTHS BEFORE YOUR MOVE

1. **Make up a budget.** Estimate the cost of your move and make a file for all moving-related paperwork (and receipts for expenses, if your move is tax deductible).

2. **Select a moving company** (see page 175, "Choosing a Mover"). Meet with your mover to go over every detail of the move, including scheduling, packing, loading, delivery, insurance coverage, claims procedures, and all costs.

3. **Weed out your belongings.** Now is the time to sort through books, clothes, furnishings, or other household items that you no longer want or need. Hold a garage sale or donate them.

4. **Repair, refurbish, dry-clean.** Send out drapes for cleaning, have carpets shampooed, repair any broken furniture or other items you've been meaning to mend.

ONE MONTH BEFORE YOUR MOVE

1. **Notify your doctor, dentist, and veterinarian** of the move and have records and prescriptions

transferred to your new city (or copied and given directly to you).

2. **Arrange for a records transfer** for anyone in the family attending school.

3. **If pets are being shipped,** call airlines and select the one you'll use; ask about required vaccinations and make a checkup appointment with the vet. If pets aren't being shipped, consider boarding them during the move.

4. **Notify your bank.** Ask if they can transfer your account to your new location or ask for banking recommendations in your new city.

5. **Cancel newspaper** and stop other deliveries.

6. **Send change of address cards** to your post office, and to magazines, creditors, friends, accountant, attorney, employers, etc.

7. **Notify insurance companies** (auto, homeowner's, health, etc.) of the move.

8. **Call the Department of Motor Vehicles** in your new city to ask about auto registration and licensing requirements.

9. **Call local utility companies** to request disconnection. Plan to leave all utilities, including the telephone, turned on until the house is empty and cleaned up. Give companies your forwarding address for any refunds due you.

10. **Arrange to have utilities connected** in your new location.

THREE WEEKS BEFORE YOUR MOVE

1. **Gather moving supplies.** See "Checklist for a Packing Kit" on page 183.

2. **Empty your safe deposit box.** Pack the contents in a box or file you will carry yourself.

3. **Start packing.** Work on one room at a time and begin by packing the items you use least often. Label boxes clearly, indicating the room and noting the contents. Put heavy items (like books) in small boxes and light ones in large.

4. **Eat up perishables.** Invite neighbors or friends over for a "leftovers" party. Serve a few drinks, as movers won't transport open liquor bottles.

5. **Dispose of flammable and combustible material.** Movers won't take these.

TWO WEEKS BEFORE YOUR MOVE

1. **Make a floor plan of your new house for the movers.** A drawing that shows them where you want the furniture will make their job go more smoothly and free you to attend to many other details.

2. **Make arrangements for a place to stay** the night your household is loaded and trucked off by the movers.

3. **Return library books and videos.** Also return neighbors' house keys and any items you may have borrowed.

4. **Arrange to have your house and yard maintained.** If the place will stand empty for any length of time, ask a neighbor to water the yard and keep an eye on the house. Notify the local police department that the home will be empty.

5. **Call gas company and other necessary serviceman** to disconnect appliances and prepare them for the move. Arrange to have them reconnected at your destination.

6. **Find homes for houseplants.** If you're making a long-distance move and can't take plants with you, distribute them to friends and neighbors.

The Week of the Move

1. **Back up your computer** and carefully pack your diskettes. Disassemble the computer, labeling cables, wires, and ports.

2. **Pack your family's "survival kit."** (See "What to Take When the Movers Take the Rest," page 184.) Label this box "Last On First Off" so the movers will know what to do with it.

3. **Pack suitcases.** Pack clothes you're not sending with the movers.

4. **Clean the refrigerator, stove, and oven.** Defrost and dry the refrigerator if it's being moved. Put charcoal or baking soda in the dishwasher and refrigerator to prevent mildew.

5. **Give movers your new address and phone number.**

6. **Label items that will stay in the old house.** Your movers may give you red tags for these items. If you're making the labels yourself, make sure they stand out clearly.

7. **Reconfirm arrangements for kennel, babysitter, pet shipping.**

8. **Buy drinks and snacks** for friends, family, and helpers on moving day. Don't forget disposable cups.

9. **Obtain payment for movers.** Depending on the terms, you may need to pay the movers with cash or traveler's checks before they unload your belong-

ings. Have tens and twenties on hand if you plan to tip them. (See "Tips on Tipping," page 132).

 ## MOVING DAY

1. **Be ready to direct movers when they arrive.**

2. **Do a final walk-through of your home** to be sure you haven't forgotten anything.

3. **Put out the trash.** After the movers leave, walk through the house again and pick up anything left behind. Put trash out on the curb.

4. **Make sure the doors and windows are locked.**

Checklist for a Packing Kit

If you are packing your household yourself, put together a kit of supplies and keep it in one place. You'll
be surprised how this will smooth and simplify what
can be a highly chaotic process. A preassembled kit will
save you from the frustration of searching everywhere
for packing tape, or discovering at midnight that you
don't have any marking pens.

1. **Boxes.** Begin collecting them from office supply,
   liquor, and other stores. Avoid grocery store boxes
   as they may harbor insects attracted by the food—or
   their eggs. Consider purchasing certain boxes from a
   moving company; wardrobe boxes, for example,
   will simplify moving the contents of your closets.

2. **Bubble wrap.**

3. **Newspapers.**

4. **Rolls of 2-inch packing tape with dispensers.**

5. **Masking tape.** Use it to fasten rolled-up rugs, to
   secure moving parts, etc. Masking tape can also be
   used to label boxes.

6. **String.** Use it to secure furniture doors or other
   items you don't want to put tape on.

7. **Small plastic bags with twist ties.** These will
   be invaluable for screws, brackets, and other miscellaneous items.

8. **Felt-tip markers.**

9. **Scissors and box cutters.**

10. **Tools.** You'll simplify life even further if you keep
    screwdrivers and a hammer in the kit so they'll be
    handy when you need to take something apart.

What to Take When the Movers Take the Rest

Pack a "survival kit" so you and your family will be comfortable in the new house until the movers arrive—or until you have the energy to unpack the moving boxes. Major moving companies recommend packing:

1. **Kitchen items.** Disposable plates, cups, and utensils. Can and bottle openers. Tea and coffee (don't forget filters and pot), aluminum foil, napkins, paper towels, sponge, and dish soap.

2. **Bedroom items.** Sheets, blankets, and pillowcases.

3. **Bathroom items.** Towels, toilet paper, soap, and toiletries.

4. **Household items.** Flashlights, scissors, light bulbs, trash bags.

5. **Tools.** Hammer, screwdrivers, pliers, nails, box opener, masking tape, and thumbtacks in case you need to put sheets over the windows as temporary curtains.

6. **Personal items.** Depending on the timing of your movers' arrival, it may be useful to take clothing, toiletries, an alarm clock, and other items you'd need overnight.

7. **First aid kit.** See page 24.

 If you make up the beds as soon as they arrive, you'll save yourself from having to do this chore when you're so exhausted all you want to do is go to sleep!

Travel

Travel usually goes most smoothly for those who've had the most experience doing it. But this expertise is usually won the hard way, by making plenty of mistakes. You can avoid learning the hard way, though, by cruising through these lists. They'll help you get organized, and you'll soon be traveling with the ease and sophistication of a seasoned pro.

✔ How to Choose a Travel Agent

Despite the sharp rise in the number of travelers purchasing their own airline tickets on the Internet, 80 percent of all flights are still booked by travel agents. Their services cost you little or nothing because they are mainly paid through commissions from airlines, hotels, car rental agencies, and so forth. Although some agents now charge a processing fee to make up for commission caps instituted in 1985 by the airlines, most are trying to give you your money's worth by offering better and more creative services. Many agencies now do specialized destination planning (they can arrange your African safari, your white-water rafting trip, or your trek through Nepal), but even for less exotic trips, a travel agent can set you up with rental cars, getaway packages, and guided tours and save you a lot of legwork.

Before you put your dream vacation or important business trip in anyone's hands, make sure you will be working with a seasoned agent who has your best interests at heart. Ask these questions at three or four agencies and take notes on the answers.

1. **Are you approved by the International Air Transport Association (IATA) and Airline Reporting Corporation (ARC)?** IATA requires bonding for membership; ARC is the organization that collects funds from travel agencies and regulates their daily operations. An agency without IATA or ARC affiliations is not a travel agency at all, merely a booking agent or tour operator.

2. **Are you a member of the American Society of Travel Agents (ASTA)?** Membership doesn't guarantee professional conduct and ethics, but ASTA has a code of principles to follow. The Society also has a mediation/arbitration system between member agencies and their customers.

3. **Are your agents Certified Travel Counselors?** The Institute of Certified Travel Agents only grants CTC status to agents who have completed a special training course and have at least five years' full-time experience. If your agent doesn't have this certification, he or she may not have the background and experience necessary to get the best deals for you.

4. **Do you have preferred supplier arrangements with any travel companies?** If your agent has such relationships and receives bonuses, rebates, or other remuneration from certain companies, you may not wind up with the best deal. On the other hand, if you suddenly need an airline seat or hotel room for an emergency trip, your agent's

relationship with "preferred suppliers" could work to your advantage. Evaluate a "yes" answer in terms of whether it might be of value to you.

5. **Does your agency subscribe to the OAG electronic tariff system?** This is a computerized version of the monthly tariff book most travel agents use. It is updated daily and allows agents to get the hottest information on special offers, such as promotional and introductory fares.

6. **Do you focus primarily on business or leisure travel?** Do you have agents who specialize in one or the other? It's wise to pick an agent who specializes in the kind of travel you do most often. You might even consider using one person at the agency for vacations and another for your business trips.

7. **Does your agency use three or more Computer Reservations Systems (CRSs)?** With fewer than three, the agency may be missing the latest and best fares. If it doesn't have access to more than one, an agency can make up for it by routinely checking last-minute seat availability with airlines for which it doesn't have direct CRS access.

8. **Does the owner work in the agency?** An owner-operated agency often runs more smoothly and has less turnover of agents. It is also good to know that if you have a problem, you can immediately take it to someone with a vested interested in keeping you happy.

9. **Do you deliver tickets and is there a charge for it?** This can be a wonderful convenience if the agency you choose is not on your normal driving route.

10. **Will you keep my travel profile on file?** A profile that includes your frequent flier numbers,

your meal and seating preferences, and any other special needs will save you time and lessen the chance of booking errors.

 Sometimes in-house travel agents at large companies will book personal travel. Check to see if your company offers this convenience.

✔ How to Pack for a Trip

The most important advice about packing for a trip can be stated simply in two words: *pack light.* Figuring out how to do that—while packing everything you need—is more complicated and takes practice. Follow the tips on this checklist and you'll pack like a veteran traveler the next time you go away.

1. **Coordinate your outfits.** Bring clothes you can mix and match. Choose one main color for your travel wardrobe, such as black, gray, navy, or khaki, and pack only items that coordinate.

2. **Consider your plans.** Make a list of your planned activities and consider which clothing will be best for each event. Remember color coordination as you do this.

3. **Figure out what you can get away with.** If you'll be seeing different people every day, take fewer items and get more use out of them by bringing clean shirts or tops to refresh a few suits, skirts, pants, and jackets.

4. **Inspect your clothes.** Don't wait until you're filling your suitcase to look at the clothes you're planning to pack. Give yourself time to sew on buttons, do laundry, or take clothes to the cleaners.

5. **Shun your shoes.** Coordinating your clothing means you'll need fewer pairs of shoes. Since they are usually the heaviest and bulkiest items in a suitcase, consider taking two pairs that can be rotated for hygiene and comfort and a third pair of casual shoes or sneakers.

6. **Avoid wrinkles.** Pack in layers that are tight enough to keep garments from shifting around and loose enough so they aren't jammed together.

- Pack suits, dresses, shirts, and blouses in plastic dry cleaning bags.
- Drape longer clothing across the suitcase and leave the edges hanging. Lay smaller items like T-shirts on top before folding the long ends over. This provides a little cushioning and helps prevent creasing.
- Roll sweaters, pajamas, and other casual clothing to fill any gaps in the suitcase.
- Put heavy items, such as shoes and hair dryer, together along one edge of the suitcase or in a separate bag to keep them from weighing down and crushing clothing.
- Forget about linen.

7. **Make a list.** Before you pack, jot down everything you must take with you. Check each item off as you put it in your luggage (don't forget to include toiletries, medication, etc.). This will do wonders to reduce travel-induced premature aging.

Tip Roll underwear, socks, and other small items and tuck them into your shoes to keep your favorite wingtips from being crushed. Put shoes in plastic bags to avoid soiling other clothing.

What to Pack in Your Carry-on

If you'd hate to lose it, pack it in your carry-on. Also, pack whatever you need for one night in case your luggage is lost or delayed. Use these ideas to create a checklist tailored to your requirements.

1. **Medication.**
2. **Eyeglasses and contact lens solution.**
3. **Expensive or irreplaceable jewelry.**
4. **Itinerary.**
5. **Tickets.**
6. **Hotel address and reservation number.**
7. **Rental car information and confirmation number.**
8. **Directions to destination.**
9. **Money and credit cards.**
10. **Overnight essentials.** If you're caught without your luggage, you'll want your toothbrush and other toiletries.
11. **Passport and visa** if needed.
12. **Reading material.**
13. **Camera, computer, and any other expensive equipment.**

✓ Before You Go Abroad: What You Need

If you are traveling to a foreign country for the first time, you may be in unfamiliar territory long before your plane takes off; it isn't easy to figure out exactly what you need to do to leave and enter another country legally. This checklist tells you what you may need and how to get it.

1. **Passport.** A United States citizen must have a current passport to leave the country. U.S. passports are good for ten years and cost $65; renewals are $55. It usually takes about six to eight weeks to process a passport, but that can be cut to about ten days by asking for the Expedite option, which costs an extra $35. First-time passport applicants must go in person to a passport office or post office with proof of citizenship (a certified copy of a birth certificate or naturalization or citizenship papers), and proof of identity (a driver's license or photo identity card). You'll also need two identical 2×2-inch front-view photos of yourself against a white or light background which you can purchase quickly and easily at most photo stores and certain copy centers. (It helps to wear a dark color when you have this photo taken.) Make a copy of your passport to carry with you, but keep it separate from the original.

2. **Visa.** A visa is an official authorization stamped inside your passport showing that the host country permits you to travel within its borders for a limited amount of time and for a specific purpose (vacation, business, academic study, etc.). Not all countries require American tourists to obtain visas. To find out if you need one for your trip and how long it will take to obtain one, call the country's embassy or

consulate in the city nearest you or the airline or hotel you've booked. But make sure your information is current; visa requirements can change quickly with new governments or during politically sensitive events.

3. **Vaccines or immunization shots.** To find out about the requirements for your destination, call the State Department at 202-647-5225 or the Centers for Disease Control at 404-639-2572. You can also check with your local health department.

4. **International driver's license.** In many countries, a valid U.S. license is sufficient for legal driving and car rental. Call the American Automobile Association to find out what is required where you are traveling. The AAA can issue the license, which costs $10, requires only a simple application form, and is issued immediately.

5. **Automobile insurance.** Call your insurance representative and ask for details on what coverage your policy provides for driving in a foreign country. Also talk to your credit card company; some offer fairly generous coverage for their customers traveling overseas. It's a good idea to bring your automobile insurance information with you in any case.

6. **Foreign currency.** Purchase foreign currency before your trip through Thomas Cook Currency Services (800-287-7362) or a foreign currency office in your area (listed in the Yellow Pages). The exchange rate is published in the Sunday travel section of most major newspapers; you can get updated information by calling a currency dealer. It's cheaper to obtain foreign currency by using your ATM to withdraw money from a bank machine in that country. But there can be glitches if you don't ask your bank

for the exact procedure ahead of time (must it come from your savings account? will your PIN number work as usual?).

7. **Telephone codes.** Call your calling card company to ask for the access numbers for the countries you'll be visiting. Also, let them know you're going overseas. Occasionally telephone calling card companies will place a "theft and loss" hold on a card that suddenly turns up in a foreign country.

✓ Extras to Pack When You Travel Abroad

Experienced travelers have a saying about packing for overseas trips: "Bring half the clothes and twice the money." Here's a checklist of the other things you'll want to take along.

1. **Passport.**

2. **Visa,** if required.

3. **Electricity converter for foreign plugs.** You'll need a 1600-watt converter.

4. **Adapters for the converter.** Electric outlets differ the world over. You'd be wise to pick up an assortment of socket adapters when you purchase the electricity converter.

5. **Foreign currency** to cover taxi or other transportation expense when you arrive.

6. **Street address and telephone number of the U.S. embassy** or consulate in your destination city.

7. **List of credit card numbers.** Make a couple of copies and take one with you, leave one at home.

8. **Emergency assistance numbers for your credit cards,** in case they are lost or stolen. Add this to the list of credit cards, but keep the number in another place just to be extra careful.

9. **Currency conversion chart.** Freelance foreign correspondent Kitty Felde suggests making one yourself before leaving home by sitting down with your calculator and the currency exchange rates from the daily newspaper. It is especially convenient for odd sums or multiple countries. Keep the chart in your wallet.

10. **Washcloths.** They aren't standard equipment all over the world. If you use them, consider packing a few.

11. **Benadryl.** This over-the-counter antihistamine usually causes drowsiness as a side effect. Many veteran travelers take Benadryl to help them sleep during overnight flights.

12. **Small book of foreign phrases.** The simplest transactions can become complicated if you have no idea how to communicate with non-English speakers.

13. **Preaddressed envelopes.** You can also print out computer labels for postcards and letters you plan to send. This method is lighter than carrying your address book and safer in case you lose it.

14. **Reentry packet.** Put everything you'll need when you get home (house and car keys, parking receipt, money for parking lot, phone calls, public transportation, etc.) in a change purse or Ziploc bag in a deep pocket of your carry-on. These items will be out of your way during the trip but right where you need them when you get home.

✓ Questions to Ask Before You Book a Hotel Room

The quality and character of your accommodations can influence the whole experience of your trip, sometimes coloring the way you feel about an entire city. Ask these questions to ensure you're getting exactly the room you want and at the best possible price.

1. **Is there a cancellation penalty?** Some hotels keep a portion of your deposit, some will refund only if they are able to book the room after you cancel, and still others will refund a deposit if the reservation is cancelled with a certain amount of notice. Make sure you understand what the policy is.

2. **Is there a check-out penalty?** Some hotels charge you for leaving before your check-out date. For example, if you book the room through Monday, but decide to leave Sunday, will you pay a fee?

3. **What are check-in and check-out times?** Is there any grace period for checking out a bit later? Is it possible to check in early, or to store your bags at the hotel if you arrive before your room is ready?

4. **What other costs may be added?** A hotel's overnight rate may sound good, but it quickly becomes expensive if you must pay substantial taxes and surcharges or high fees to garage your car each day. (These fees may not apply at lodgings outside major cities, so you may want to consider staying beyond city limits.)

5. **What is your confirmation policy?** If you arrive late in the day, until what time will the hotel hold your room? Does your deposit guarantee it for you?

6. **What is nearby?** Ask where the hotel is relative to the activities you plan for your visit (going to the

beach, visiting museums, exploring the historic district, going to the theater). Even if you will have a car, it's good to know how much time is required to get where you want to go.

7. **Are the facilities modern?** Many older hotels absolutely ooze charm. But when the shower oozes rusty water, the charm dries up fast. Ask what you're getting into when booking older accommodations.

8. **What amenities do you offer?** Do you prefer a swimming pool? Workout area? Do the rooms have telephones and televisions? How about hair dryers? The answers to these questions will definitely affect your packing decisions and could have an impact on whether or not you're happy there.

9. **Do you have discounts available?** You may be eligible for discounts based on your age, membership in associations such as AAA, or your frequent flyer status. But you won't know if you don't ask.

10. **May I have a confirmation number?** This will be invaluable if the hotel "can't find" your reservation when you arrive.

SPECIFY **EXACTLY WHAT YOU WANT**   Don't take anything for granted when booking a hotel. If you want a king-sized bed in a non-smoking room and you can't bear street noise, tell the reservation agent.

 Avoid calling a hotel chain's toll-free 800 reservation number. You'll almost always get a better deal by telephoning the hotel directly and dealing with a clerk at the desk who will have more information about specials and more leeway to offer lower rates.

✓ **C**hecklist for Staying Safe at a Hotel

The key to protecting yourself and your possessions while traveling is not very different from staying safe at home: be alert to your surroundings and use common sense in evaluating situations that come up. Put this checklist in your luggage for reference while traveling and review it before you leave home.

1. **Safety in numbers.** If you're a woman traveling alone, consider booking the room and checking in as husband and wife. To avoid a double room charge, phone the desk shortly after your arrival to let them know that "Mr." won't be coming after all.

2. **Study the fire exit plan** posted on the back of the door. If nothing is posted, make a note of the exits nearest your room and spend a couple of moments planning a quick exit route, just in case.

3. **Don't attract attention.** Avoid displaying large amounts of cash, jewelry, or other valuables at the registration desk, hotel restaurant, or lobby.

4. **Keep your door shut.** Use your peep hole to find out who's at the door before opening it. Never open the door to anyone claiming to be a hotel service person unless you've called for one. If in doubt, telephone the desk to confirm the identity while the person waits outside the door. A rubber doorjamb—the kind used to keep doors open—also works well to keep doors closed when it's wedged under the inside. Make sure any connecting or sliding glass doors and windows are securely locked.

5. **Don't hang the "Make Up This Room" card** on your door when you go out. It's an invitation to burglars looking for easy pickings. Leaving the "Do

Not Disturb" sign up and the television on can be a fairly good deterrent. If the maid passes you by, you can always call housekeeping later in the day.

6. **Avoid regular patterns of entering and leaving your room.** Vary the times at which you leave and return and occasionally come back to your room after a few minutes, if possible.

7. **Be alert for staged distractions** in the lobby that may be created to provide an opportunity for a pickpocket or purse/luggage snatcher.

8. **Hand carry** your precious items and vital documents. Keep your laptop, personal travel documents, and anything else you can't afford to lose under your own control at all times.

9. **Use the room or hotel safe.** Don't leave anything valuable behind when you exit the room.

10. **Use the main entrance** to your hotel when returning after dark. Avoid dimly lit garages without security patrols. In any type of parking structure, look around for strange or suspicious behavior before you get out of the car.

11. **Purchase an instant release key chain** so you can keep your house and other keys when you leave your car key with valets or other parking personnel.

12. **Keep your room key** where it can't be stolen.

Health

Your know that your health is important, of course, but life is hectic and it's easy to let health maintenance slide unless something goes wrong. These checklists will help you take control of your own good health by giving you the information you need to do it. They'll guide you in important (but occasionally baffling) matters such as finding a good doctor and selecting an exercise plan.

Choosing a Primary Care Physician

If you can manage the time, it's a good idea to schedule a get-acquainted visit with a few doctors before you commit yourself to one. As always, start by asking friends and family for recommendations. Then call several physicians in your insurance plan to find out if they're taking new patients. Schedule a short visit and offer to pay for the time. This investment will pay dividends if it helps you find a doctor you trust and feel comfortable with.

QUESTIONS TO ASK BEFORE YOU SCHEDULE A VISIT

1. **Where did the doctor go to school?** Did he go to a reputable medical school? Did she complete three years of residency training in her advertised area of expertise? The AMA has an on-line service called "Doctor Finder" (www.ama-assn.org), where you can check education and training on any licensed physician in the country.

2. **Is the doctor board-certified for her type of practice?** Board certification means the doctor has received advanced training and passed rigorous qualifying exams. But some doctors may emphasize board certification and fail to mention that it's in a field they no longer do much work in. To check board certification on a physician you're considering, call the American Board of Medical Specialties at 800-776-CERT (2378) or go to its website at www.certifieddoctor.org.

3. **What hospitals is the doctor affiliated with?** Is one of them convenient to your home? Does it have a good reputation?

QUESTIONS TO ASK AT THE DOCTOR'S OFFICE

1. **Am I comfortable with the doctor's staff?** The way you are treated by the staff makes a big difference to your experience with the doctor, of course. And it's often a reliable indication of the doctor's concern for patients as people, rather than as bodies. Pay attention to the atmosphere behind the reception desk: Does the staff seem efficient? Are they helpful in person and on the telephone?

2. **Do you require full payment from me or will you wait for direct payment from my insurance company?** There isn't necessarily a right answer to this (unless you're on Medicare, in which case the doctor should wait to be paid by them). It's a matter of your preference and financial situation.

QUESTIONS FOR THE DOCTOR

1. **What is your approach to health care?** Is the doctor oriented toward prevention? Does he ask questions about your lifestyle and health habits and discuss various ways you might improve your health? Does he see himself as your partner, collaborating with you on achieving your health and well-being?

2. **What happens when you're away?** Ask the doctor who covers for her when she's on vacation and during weekends and days off. Ask why the person has been selected and don't be afraid to quiz the doctor about the substitute's credentials.

3. **How often will I need checkups?** The answer to this question should be based on your age, general health, and medical and family history.

4. **What tests do you regularly order and what do you check for?** Does the doctor explain the tests and the reason for doing them in a way that's easy to understand?

5. **Can I bring a family member or friend into the examination room?** This is a reasonable request and your primary care physician should be open to it if you'd like to do it.

Over-Forty checkups: What You Need When

After age forty most men and women begin to find out what it means to "feel your age." Those little signs that you're not a kid anymore—tiring more easily, having a harder time taking off weight—aren't serious. But they are reminders that we take our health for granted at the risk of losing it. If you're over forty, talk to your doctor about scheduling the exams on this checklist.

 FOR MEN AND WOMEN

1. **Blood pressure.** Test at least every two years. But you needn't go that long, since blood pressure checks can be part of any routine exam or trip to your doctor.

2. **Cholesterol blood test.** Test every five years for total and HDL count; every three to five years after age sixty-five.

3. **Fecal occult blood test.** Test annually for blood in feces, which may be an indication of colon cancer or other gastrointestinal problems.

4. **Colorectal cancer screenings.** Screen every five to ten years. Each exam should include sigmoidoscopy, colonoscopy, barium enema, digital rectal exam.

5. **Fasting plasma glucose.** Screen for diabetes every three years, if you're overweight or have a family history of diabetes.

6. **Skin exam.** In addition to a monthly self-exam, see a doctor annually to detect early skin cancers.

7. **Eye exam.** Examine every two years, or annually if you have diabetes or a family history of macular degeneration.

8. **Dental checkup.** Schedule regular cleanings, as recommended by your dentist.

 ## FOR WOMEN

1. **Mammogram.** Schedule annually or every other year, depending on your doctor's opinion.
2. **Pelvic exam and PAP test.** Schedule every year. (Sixty percent of cervical cancers are diagnosed in women between the ages of fifty and seventy.)
3. **Bone density test.** Have your first one at age fifty, or sooner if you are in a high-risk category (Asian or Caucasian, small boned, low calcium intake, heavy drinking or smoking, family history of osteoporosis).

 ## FOR MEN

1. **Digital rectal exam.** To check for prostate cancer every year.
2. **Prostate specific antigen (PSA) test.** This test has been controversial, so discuss it with your doctor.

How to Join a Gym Without Straining Your Wallet

If you'd like to exercise at a gym, but are scared off by hefty sign-up fees and lengthy contracts, throw on your workout clothes and exercise these tips!

1. **Think car shopping.** Just as you wouldn't think of paying sticker price for the car you buy, you shouldn't take a health club's advertised price at face value. Most health clubs are eager to sell memberships—and that gives you some bargaining power.

2. **Shop early in the year.** Club owners know that the combination of post-holiday guilt, new year's optimism, and low prices can send scores of exercisers their way. Many gym managers make sign-up as irresistible as possible in January, offering bargain rates and flexible terms.

3. **Shop around.** Spending the time to compare costs at several clubs in your area will pay off in the long run. If you can tell one manager that the club across town will give you a better rate, he may try to match or beat that price.

4. **Be bold.** Ask for the sign-up rate the club offered last summer or last month, even if it has expired. If they want your business, they may be happy to give you a discount.

5. **Bargain.** Offer *them* something. For example, if your schedule permits, promise you won't use the club during their peak hours (usually 6 to 8 A.M. and 4 to 8 P.M. weekdays).

6. **Look for flexible terms.** Most clubs make their money by locking you in with a large initiation fee

or a long-term contract. This is highly profitable for the clubs because many people stop attending after the first couple of months—but the club still gets its money. Look for the flexibility of month-to-month contracts, the ability to transfer your membership if you move or lose interest, or refunds in case of moving or illness.

7. **Don't say yes too quickly.** Salespeople often pressure club shoppers to sign "now" to take advantage of a discount. Don't be fooled. Hold out for the terms you want (a one-year contract, rather than a three-year, for example) because you can probably get them.

8. **Bring a friend.** Most clubs will reward a new member who refers a friend or give a special rate to friends who join at the same time. Ask about these specials.

9. **Get a group rate.** Many companies arrange for group fitness discounts for employees who join a specific gym. If your company doesn't, ask the gym what you could do to get a group organized.

✔ **How to Choose a Health Club You'll Use**

No matter what kind of deal you get signing up for a
health club, you'll have wasted your money if you stop
going after a few months. Take your time to inspect the
club and evaluate its features to make sure it meets your
needs.

1. **Handy location.** Chances are you won't use a
   club that's not easily accessible, no matter how good
   your intentions are. Narrow your choices to clubs
   within comfortable distance of home or work.

2. **Activities and scheduling.** What hours is the
   pool open for lap swimming? How far in advance
   must you reserve tennis, basketball, or racquetball
   courts? Look over the club's printed schedule for
   yoga, aerobics, or other classes you're interested in.
   If you want to do aerobics on your way to work, but
   classes don't start until 8:00 A.M., this club may not
   work for you. Find out how often the schedule of
   activities changes and how likely you are to get into
   a class you want. Do you need a reservation? Do
   you have to pay extra for certain classes?

3. **Reciprocity.** Does your membership include use
   of other clubs in the area? If you travel frequently,
   will your membership allow you to use clubs in
   other states?

4. **Equipment, facilities, and maintenance.**
   Don't be taken in by a salesperson's claim that bro-
   ken equipment or shabby facilities are about to un-
   dergo a transformation. Judge by what you see.
   - Is all the equipment functioning?
   - Does the equipment look shabby or old?
   - Is the pool clean?
   - How clean are the shower and locker room? Do
     they smell clean?

- Are the temperature and humidity comfortable in the exercise areas?

5. **Elbow room.** Go to the club during prime time and notice crowding in classes and in workout areas. If you'll be using the club during off hours, visit then and see how crowded it is.

6. **Staff.** Ask about the training and experience of staff members. Some certifications to look for: AFAA, the Aerobics and Fitness Association of America; ACSM, the American Council on Exercise; and the Cooper Institute for Aerobics Research. Certification from these institutions doesn't guarantee competence, but it's a start. Talk to some of the instructors and judge their knowledge and communication skills yourself.

7. **Atmosphere.** If you feel uncomfortable—whether the music is too loud, the other members seem too young, or there's just an overload of flashy Lycra outfits—you may wind up avoiding the place.

✓ Ten Ways to Get Exercise Without Being Miserable

You don't have to lift weights at a gym or run five miles a day to keep yourself fit. Just changing a few sedentary habits will contribute to your fitness and maybe even shift your attitude about exercise. Here are ten ideas to get you moving.

1. **Shun elevators.** Make it a point to use the stairs instead of pushing that "Up" arrow every time. It is better for your body—and your morale—not to overdo it. Start with one or two flights at a time and add more flights only when it feels comfortable.

2. **Park your car far away . . .** You'll get significantly more movement into the day, and avoid that frustrating and time-wasting experience of searching for a "good" parking place.

3. **. . . And keep it parked.** If you have to drive downtown for a few errands, park and leave the car. If you're collecting several parcels, walk back to the car to drop them off before you go on to your next errand on foot.

4. **Do two things at once.** Add exercise to your everyday activities by stretching and doing leg or arm lifts while you talk on the telephone, brush your teeth, or dry your hair. If you have a cordless phone, walk while you talk.

5. **Dance the dust away.** Housecleaning will be a bit more fun (and a decent aerobic workout) if you play danceable CDs while you work. (See "Cleaning Supplies" on page 86.)

6. **Play with your kids.** And I don't mean video games. Get out there and bike or skate with them,

walk up and down the soccer field at practices, climb the slide and use the swings at the playground!

7. **Take the long way.** Don't use the closest bathroom. Walk around the block to get where you're going. Put a little distance between yourself and your destination.

8. **Make a walking date.** Do you have a local friend you'd like to spend more time with? Suggest that you both get up an hour earlier and meet for a morning walk. Even twenty minutes of striding and arm swinging will do you good.

9. **Buy a bike.** Unless you live in an extremely hilly area, taking a bike ride is an appealing and moderate way to exercise. Consider running errands on your bike—it might make you feel like a kid again!

10. **Go East.** Many confirmed couch potatoes have been converted after trying such Eastern practices as yoga or tai chi. These meditative and gentle movements enhance both physical and spiritual well-being.

The Law

The lists in this section fall under the "read it now in case you need to know it later" category. Most of us would be just as happy never to encounter the legal system, but in case you do, having the information in these lists will make a scary situation a lot less scary.

☑ When to Call a Lawyer

They usually cost a lot of money to hire. Their integrity is mocked in scores of jokes. In general, the world loves to hate them. But sometimes there's no way around it: you just have to call a lawyer. It isn't possible to foresee every scenario, but the attorneys who assisted in the preparation of this checklist advise you to call one of their colleagues if:

1. **You are arrested or charged with a crime** or learn that you are being investigated by the government.
2. **You are served with a search warrant.**
3. **You receive any document that directs you to respond** or to appear in court, or before any government agency. These include: subpoena, summons, complaint, or arbitration demand.

4. **You are in an automobile accident resulting in injury** to persons or property.

5. **You have been hurt or your property has been damaged** by someone else.

6. **You have a dispute with an insurance company** over payment of a claim.

7. **You have been treated unfairly by an individual or a business** and it has caused you financial loss.

8. **You are contemplating getting a divorce, adopting a child,** or are having problems with child support or visitation.

9. **You are a victim of domestic violence,** or your child has been abused.

10. **Your special needs child is not receiving proper or adequate educational services** from your public school.

11. **You are concerned about an alcoholic, drug-addicted, mentally ill,** aged, or disabled family member, relation, or friend who needs governmental services.

12. **You believe that someone is asserting or has asserted undue influence** over the decisions or financial affairs of a family member or relative.

13. **You want to have a will, trust, or estate plan drawn up,** or if a relative dies leaving you an inheritance.

14. **You are contemplating filing for bankruptcy.**

15. **You have been terminated from employment** or demoted for reporting a violation of the law.

16. **You believe you are being discriminated against** in the workplace based on race, gender, na-

tional origin, age, religion, sexual orientation, or because of a disability or illness.

17. **You are being subjected to a hostile working environment** as a result of the conduct of other employees, supervisor(s), or your employer.

18. **You have a problem involving real estate,** such as with a landlord or tenant, a boundary dispute, or a zoning or other land-use violation.

19. **You want to buy or sell a business or real estate,** or are involved in a complicated real estate transaction, especially in an area subject to governmental regulation.

20. **You want to challenge the actions of a government official.**

21. **You believe your rights have been violated** by an individual or by a government agency.

22. **You are not receiving benefits or services** for which you have applied, or believe that you are entitled to receive from the government.

23. **You believe that a governmental agency is not effectively enforcing the laws** with respect to someone else's activities and this has an impact on you or your property.

24. **You want to obtain a patent or copyright.**

25. **You want to know what your legal rights, duties, and obligations are** with respect to a specific situation.

26. **You are advised to do so by another professional,** such as an accountant, tax, or financial adviser.

Questions to Ask Before Choosing a Lawyer

The first step in hiring a lawyer is to come up with a list of prospects recommended by people you know and trust. In addition to your family and friends, ask professionals such as your accountant, doctor, or financial planner for recommendations. Your state bar association may be able to give you a list of lawyers in your area, but understand that the bar association is only passing along names, not making recommendations. Once you have a list of candidates, use these questions to check the credentials, experience, and compatibility of those you are considering. You can't ascertain compatibility by asking specific questions, but take into account the way the lawyer relates to you in the telephone and in-person interviews.

ON THE TELEPHONE

Start with a phone call to find out which attorneys may be worth the time (and possibly the money) involved in a face-to-face meeting. Describe clearly and briefly why you're seeking legal assistance and ask questions that focus on the attorney's suitability for handling your case.

1. **Have you handled this type of case before?**
2. **How many years have you practiced?**
3. **What kinds of cases do you handle most often?**
4. **Is there a fee for the initial (in person) consultation?** If so, how much?
5. **Do you sign a written fee agreement with clients?**

6. **What are your rates for this type of case?** Are your fees negotiable?

7. **Would you be the lawyer actually working on my case?** (Sometimes you'll be talking to a partner who's adept at "selling" the firm, but will hand your case over to a staff attorney. You may not want to sign on with a firm that doesn't let you interview your potential lawyer on the telephone.)

8. **May I have the names and phone numbers of clients you've represented with cases like mine?** Before you schedule in-person interviews with the lawyers who pass muster over the telephone, call your state bar to find out if any have been publicly disciplined and to confirm that they are licensed to practice law in your state.

 IN PERSON

An in-person interview can then help you determine whether the lawyer is experienced enough and willing to take your case, what services the lawyer will perform and how much you will be charged, and whether you and the lawyer communicate well. Prepare a brief summary of the facts and dates relevant to your case and take it, along with any pertinent paperwork and documents, to each interview.

1. **What are the strengths and weaknesses of my case?** What is the likely result of my suit?

2. **Might the case go to trial?** Be settled out of court? How much could I win? What might I lose?

3. **What percentage of your cases have been like mine?** What percentage of those have had favorable outcomes?

4. **Can you describe some of those experiences for me?**

5. **How long, from start to finish, do you think this case might take?**

6. **How are your fees calculated?** What is my total bill likely to be?

7. **Do you require a retainer** (up-front payment)? How much?

8. **May I have an itemized bill?** (You have a right to ask for details on your charges.)

9. **Will you consult me prior to taking action or making important decisions on my case?**

10. **How closely will we be in touch during the process?** How often might I be hearing from you?

 **Preparing for Traffic Court**

Many people are reluctant to fight traffic tickets, even if they suspect they're in the right. They'll pay the fine by mail, which amounts to pleading guilty to a misdemeanor moving violation, just to avoid the hassle of going to traffic court. But since moving violations (as opposed to citations for mechanical defects or illegal parking) can damage your driving record and hike your insurance rates, showing up in court may be worth the trouble. Here are some tips from a veteran police officer on how to minimize your losses.

1. **Be respectful.** No matter how angry or resentful you may feel, don't go into the courtroom with a chip on your shoulder.

2. **If it's serious, hire an attorney.** If you've been charged with reckless driving or another serious moving violation, you'll be better off with an attorney. Without one, it is simply your word against the officer's, and the chance of persuading the judge in your favor is slim.

3. **Bring documentation.** If you've been charged with speeding and you plan to throw yourself on the mercy of the court because your speedometer was broken, bring proof that you've had it recalibrated to court. Just showing up and claiming your speedometer didn't work won't get you anywhere.

4. **Flaunt your good behavior.** If you have a clean driving record, and can plead extenuating circumstances, you may be able to ask the judge for a lesser offense. Use steps 1 through 3 to help you do this. If you have a long list of traffic offenses, just pay the ticket.

✓ **P**reparing for Small Claims Court

Small claims courts exist to provide quick and accessible legal resolution for disputes about relatively small amounts of money. Rules governing small claims vary from state to state—for example, the maximum amount you can sue for varies from about $1,000 in Virginia to $5,000 in California.

Speed and informality are the best things about small claims court. The entire process from filing a claim to receiving a judgment usually takes only a few weeks, while the complicated legal maneuverings in civil court proceedings may stretch over years. Some states keep small claims courts so informal that they prohibit lawyers from participating. In any case, it's rarely cost-effective to hire a lawyer for these disputes, given the small sums at stake and the high hourly fees usually charged by attorneys. It's not difficult to represent yourself, as long as you prepare carefully. Consult a legal guide for explanation of your state's laws, and use this list to help you get organized.

1. **Begin by sending a letter** to the person or company with whom you have a dispute. Make the letter brief and clear, outlining the issues and the response you expect. This is called the "demand letter" and may get you results without going to court. At the very least, it provides a clear statement of your claim and shows you tried to resolve it with the other party.

2. **Save every item related to your case.** The judge will make a decision based upon the evidence presented by both sides, not on what is said. Correspondence, bills, receipts, photographs, letters from experts—anything that can document your version

of the truth—will determine the outcome of your claim.

3. **Call your county clerk** to find out which court you must use to file your claim. (You may be required to go to a court near the defendant's home or business.)

4. **File your claim** with the small claims clerk. Call the clerk's office to ask when the clerk is available before you make the trip. Also ask about filing fees—how much they are and whether you must pay with cash.

5. **Take a copy of the demand letter** and all the documentation related to your case when you meet with the clerk. These will help the clerk assist you in drafting the complaint.

6. **Don't hesitate to ask the clerk for advice** on how to file the suit. His job is to help people use the system and he should be happy to work with you.

7. **Be on time for court,** but don't be surprised if you have to wait.

8. **Ask your witnesses to arrive promptly.**

9. **Have a carefully prepared written summary** in addition to your documentary evidence. Write it all out ahead of time so you don't lose your train of thought or forget important details when explaining your side to the judge. The proceedings are informal, but you'll still need to be concise and persuasive.

Your Money

15

Financial expert Jane Bryant Quinn sums up her advice for handling money in three sentences: "Use common sense. The simplest choices are the best ones. Impulse is your enemy, time your friend." That doesn't sound complicated, but following this advice is easier said than done. The lists in this section will give you the information you need to follow Quinn's tips on using common sense and making good choices, but you'll have to bring your own resources to the job of resisting impulses!

✓ How to Choose a Bank

Choosing a bank is like shopping for most things. First you decide what features are important to you, then start comparison shopping. Pick up brochures listing services and fees from a few banks and carefully compare them against one another. Keep your eye on the following:

1. **Ask about balance requirements.** What's the minimum balance you must maintain to avoid paying fees and to earn interest? Customers who don't regularly maintain high checking account balances

can wind up paying hefty fees for the privilege of letting the bank hold their money.

2. **Weigh the fees against freebies.** Never mind the toasters. Which free or low-cost services are most important to you? If you use ATMs regularly, look for banks that allow free unlimited ATM use. Pay attention to charges for using ATMs at other banks. Does the bank you're considering impose a fee on top of the one the other bank charges? Does the bank offer low-cost overdraft protection? Does it charge its customers for traveler's checks? If the pamphlets don't answer these questions, jot them down so you can ask when you go to the bank.

3. **Look out for your interest.** Don't be too quickly seduced by banks paying higher interest rates on checking accounts. Compare the banks' methods of calculating interest. The fairest method is to pay compound interest on your daily balance. This means you earn interest—including the previously accumulated interest—every day. Watch banks that pay:
   • Interest on your balance only after your deposit checks have cleared.
   • Interest on your lowest balance, so that if you have $3,000 in for twenty-nine days and withdraw all but $100 on the thirtieth day, you'd receive interest only on $100.
   • What appear to be generous interest rates, but on closer inspection turn out to be calculated in the bank's favor (for example, on your lowest balance). These "high" rates won't be as good a deal as a lower rate paid on your daily balance.

4. **Watch for service charges.** You could wind up losing money each month if you earn $1.70 in interest but pay $10 in ATM transactions and service charges.

5. **Don't limit your search.** Since many transactions can be handled long-distance through ATMs and on-line banking, your choice of banks needn't be limited to those in your immediate area. If you aren't happy with the offerings of neighborhood banks, feel free to look farther afield.

6. **Forgo the frills.** Some banks offer lower-cost "no frills" checking accounts designed for customers who keep a low balance and don't write many checks. If you fit that profile, find a bank that offers this option. Usually, a no-frills account allows you to write a certain number of checks (ten to fifteen) for free, charging you by the item as you go above that number.

7. **Ask for ways to save money.** Will the bank reduce fees or service charges for checking accounts for customers who maintain a savings account, purchase a CD, or take out a loan with the bank? Ask if you can reduce your monthly service charge by opting not to receive your cancelled checks with your statement, or by banking exclusively on-line or with the ATM.

8. **Customer service counts.** Higher interest rates are attractive, but the few extra dollars you earn on an account may not be as valuable in the long run if they come at the expense of friendly, personalized service when you need assistance.

9. **Visit in person.** Once you've narrowed your choice of banks, make an appointment with the new accounts clerk. This is your opportunity to gauge the bank's level of customer service and the helpfulness of its staff. To avoid unpleasant surprises, ask for a detailed list of charges you might have to pay with the account. If the person you're meeting with can't provide one, or gives vague or unclear information, move on.

How to Balance Your Checkbook

Don't be intimidated: balancing your checkbook does not require a degree in advanced bookkeeping! Balancing your account involves nothing more than comparing your checking balance with the bank's balance and making sure they both reflect the same transactions. Take it one step at a time and it won't hurt a bit.

1. **Go through your check register** and make a list of the checks you wrote that have not yet cleared. These are called "outstanding checks."

2. **Add up the dollar amounts** of all the outstanding checks.

3. **Make a list of any deposits** you made that are not yet shown on the bank statement.

4. **Add up all the fees** and charges against your account, including any ATM withdrawals and charges and automatic withdrawals (house payment, gym membership, etc.) that you hadn't entered. Subtract these amounts from your register balance.

5. **Add interest to your register balance,** plus any other credits shown on your statement but not yet written in your checkbook. This is your up-to-date checking account balance.

6. **Update the bank's balance shown** on your bank statement by adding any deposits you've made that the bank has not yet posted.

7. **Subtract the total amount of outstanding checks** from the statement balance. The bank's balance should now match the one you arrived at after adding interest and subtracting fees from your checkbook register.

8. If they don't match:

- Check the math in your check register (this is the most frequent culprit) when accounts don't balance.
- Check to see if the amount of each check and deposit matches the amount the bank actually subtracted from or added to your account. (You may have entered the amount incorrectly in your check register, or the bank may have misread your writing.)
- Look over your deposits to verify that they're properly credited to your account.
- Compare the checks listed on your bank statement with your checkbook to see if you forgot to enter a check.
- If your account still doesn't balance, notify the bank in writing immediately.

✓ Questions to Ask Before You Choose an Accountant

If your income is high enough and your tax needs complex, you may want to hire an accountant to help you with your tax preparation, as well as tax planning, budgeting, and advice on major decisions that could affect your tax standing. To find the person who best fits your needs, ask the questions on this checklist before you make your final choice.

1. **How much do you push the envelope?** Question candidates about their philosophy regarding deductions. Ask if they're likely to be proactive on your behalf, or whether they tend to be conservative. (At the same time, ask yourself which style makes you most comfortable.)

2. **What's your fee structure?** When you take your taxes to a CPA firm, your work may be handled by a variety of people and charged at different levels. Simple portions of your return may be given to staff members whose work is billed at a much lower rate. Expect to pay the CPA from $150 to $250 an hour, depending on where you live and how big a firm you're dealing with. Ask how much preparation of your return will cost and find out how each level of service will be charged.

3. **Can we talk?** Will your accountant answer questions over the telephone during the year? Some professionals will hit you with a per-hour charge for these calls; some consider the occasional call to be part of the ongoing relationship.

4. **What's your background?** As with any professional you hire, you'll want to find out how long this person has practiced, where she's worked, and what kind of training she's had. Ask about her spe-

cial areas of expertise to find out whether they match your needs.

5. **Are you selling anything?** The only thing you want your accountant to sell you is expert tax preparation and advice. Walk away from accountants who also sell investments for which they earn commissions.

6. **Will you be there if I'm audited?** Don't assume that your accountant will stay by your side if the IRS decides to audit your tax return. Ask your candidates directly whether they can and will represent you. Expect to pay extra for their time if they do.

Tip If your tax return is a bit complex, but you don't want to hire an accountant, consider hiring an "enrolled agent." These highly trained individuals will cost less than a CPA, but can give you tax advice and are licensed to represent you with the IRS in case of an audit. Many are former IRS agents. For a local referral, call the National Association of Enrolled Agents at 800-424-4339.

✓ Questions to Ask Before You Choose a Financial Planner

Begin the process of selecting a financial planner by asking yourself what you want this person to accomplish for you. Are you looking for answers about cash management and budgeting? About choosing a retirement plan or making other specific investments? Or do you want advice on your overall financial picture, including tax and estate planning, insurance needs, and a review of your financial goals? When you know what you want, you'll be better able to evaluate a prospective planner's ability to respond to your needs.

Ask friends or colleagues for names of planners they've found helpful. Your accountant or attorney may also be excellent sources. Call some of the lists below for names of qualified advisers in your area. Pose these questions to candidates before making a final decision.

1. **How are you compensated?** Financial planners generally make their money in one of two ways. Commission-based planners profit only when they sell you financial products. Fee-only planners are paid for the advice they give you, not on any products they may advise you to purchase. Many experts, including personal finance guru Jane Bryant Quinn, warn against commission-based planners who may do less planning and more selling and are likely to recommend the highest-commission products going.

   Some planners work on a combined fee-commission plan, but this arrangement can still present a conflict of interest since they will make money through their sales commission whether or not you make money through the investment. Make sure you understand exactly how the planner's fees will be calculated and whether you will make a one-time payment or will be charged periodically.

2. **Do you have a resume or printed handout describing your professional background?** You should review this carefully to make sure the planner is really a planner and not an insurance agent trying to sell you a policy or a stockbroker looking for commissions on sales.

3. **What are your professional credentials?** There is no such thing as a license to practice financial planning, and no credential guarantees competence or special talent for investing. But certain letters after a planner's name ensure that he or she has met specific standards (see below). Also find out where the person went to school and what she majored in. You don't have to rule out English or biology majors, but a background in accounting, finance, business, or law might be more reassuring.

4. **Are you registered with the SEC?** Every planner must be registered as an investment adviser with the Securities and Exchange Commission. A yes to this question is a basic requirement.

5. **May I have your CRD number?** The Central Registration Depository is maintained by the National Association of Securities Dealers (NASD). When you have the CRD number, call NASD to request a free report on the planner's licensing and employment background and possible disciplinary history. The number is 1-800-289-9999. Or review this history yourself at www.nasdr.com.

6. **How long have you been in business?** Your money and your future are on the line. Don't put them in the hands of anyone who's new to the business. Hire a planner with at least ten years' experience. This increases the likelihood that you'll be

working with a seasoned professional who has seen
the stock market go through a few cycles. You can
double-check these answers through the NASD (see
above).

7. **What is your investment philosophy?** You
want to know how this person makes investment
decisions: What is her idea of a balanced portfolio?
Does she lean more toward certain instruments—
stocks, mutual funds, real estate, etc.? What does
she think are the most significant factors in assembling successful portfolios (market timing? luck?
past performance?)? If you don't understand this
answer completely, ask for clarification. If you still
don't understand, this adviser's not for you.

8. **How do you choose the products you recommend?** Does the planner personally research everything he recommends? Does he require a certain
track record for an investment before he recommends it?

9. **Do you specialize in certain professions?**
Some planners focus their practice on entrepre-
neurs, physicians, teachers, upper-income families,
and so on. Depending on your profession, you may
be better off with someone who has experience
working with people like you.

10. **May I have names and numbers of five
clients with whom you've worked for at
least three years?** When you phone the references, ask what the planner has done for them and
whether results lived up to their expectations. Compare their experiences to the claims the planner has
made to you. Do not even consider a planner who
can't or won't give you references of current clients.

11. **Will you base your planning for me on my
personal circumstances?** You shouldn't settle for

a generic financial blueprint. You want someone who will gather complete information about your financial situation, spending habits, and long- and short-term goals. These details are critical to obtaining a plan you can live with.

12. **How often will we meet to discuss my financial situation?** There is no correct answer, but if the planner is overseeing your entire portfolio, quarterly progress meetings are a must.

13. **And ask yourself: Is this person easy to talk to? A good listener?** The planner you choose will be learning some fairly personal things about you. Not only will she know your annual income, your net worth, your dreams for your children, and your plans for retirement, she may also become familiar with your spending habits, your (and your spouse's) attitude about money, and other potentially emotional topics.

WHERE TO GO FOR MORE INFORMATION

• **NAPFA,** the National Association of Personal Financial Advisors, is composed of fee-only planners. Members of this organization have complied with all state and federal regulations, most have considerable education and experience in their field, and all participate in continuing education. NAPFA will send you a list of fee-only planners in your area (888-333-6659).

• **The Institute of Certified Financial Planners** (ICFP) issues and regulates certified financial planners. This Denver-based institute requires a comprehensive certification exam, continuing education classes, three to five years' experience in the field, and adherence to the Board's Code of Ethics. The ICFP includes both fee-only and commission-based planners. Call for names of CFPs in your area (800-282-7526).

- **The American Institute of Certified Public Accountants** (AICPA) has a program for training CPAs to do financial planning. They'll send you a list of people in your area who have the Accredited Personal Financial Specialist (APFS or PFS) designation. (Call 212-596-6200, or write to them at 1211 Avenue of the Americas, New York, NY 10036.)

- **The Association for Investment Management and Research** (AIMR) regulates chartered financial analysts. Members of this group (CFAs) are highly regarded for their considerable experience in investment decision making. They must adhere to strict rules and codes of conduct set by the AIMR and have passed three rigorous board examinations. This credential is often held by mutual fund portfolio managers and other institutional investment portfolio managers (804-980-3668).

- **The American College** in Bryn Mawr, Pennsylvania, issues the Chartered Financial Consultant designation (ChFC). This is an insurance industry designation, which signals you that these planners will focus first on selling insurance investment products. The designation requires rigorous coursework, adherence to a code of ethics, and a minimum of three years' related experience in one of several financial fields (610-526-1000).

✅ Choosing a Method for Stock Trading

The explosive growth of on-line trading has brought major changes to the brokerage business over the last few years. There are now well over a hundred on-line trading firms, including both the scrappy new Internet companies and the offspring of Wall Street's oldest and best-known houses, offering the investor more choices than ever in selecting a way to trade stock. Whether you choose a traditional brokerage or an on-line version, put your potential broker through the same careful screening you would when hiring any expert. A few things to remember as you choose:

1. **Don't confuse brokers with financial planners.** Although full-service brokerage houses provide information along with their advice, they may not tell you whether buying any stock is the wisest use of your money. Remember that all brokers are in business to make money for themselves first, and you second—maybe. This is not to say they're dishonest; it's just the way the game is played

2. **Know what you're paying for.** Full-service brokerage firms like Merrill Lynch, Shearson Lehman, and Prudential cost more per trade than discount and on-line brokerages. The higher fee buys you information about market trends, suggestions about what to buy when, and general advising and handholding through the investment process. There's no guarantee that trading through a full-service broker will net a larger return on your investment, but it does spare you the trouble of following the market yourself. Of course, you must still pay close attention to how the broker is handling your money and whether you're satisfied with the results.

3. **Not all discount brokers are the same.** Jane Bryant Quinn classifies discount brokers as either "business class or coach." "Business class" discount brokers are known as the Big Three: Charles Schwab & Co., Fidelity, and Quick and Reilly. The Big Three offer essentially the same products and services as the full-service firms, but don't give advice on what to buy. The "coach" firms offer the deepest discounts (they charge an average of 73 percent below the full-service firms and 41 percent less than the Big Three) but they only execute trades and don't offer other services. They are mainly used by seasoned stock investors who know exactly what they want and require only the transaction itself.

4. **Look at e-trading.** Placing buy and sell orders over the Internet is a very popular way to trade stocks and may become the primary way to execute such transactions. On-line trading doesn't entirely eliminate the "middle man," because you still must open a brokerage account before you can begin trading, and you pay a fee for transactions. But it could be your least expensive, most flexible trading option. When evaluating on-line trading firms pay special attention to:
   - How swiftly the firm executes trades.
   - The level of advice that's offered (if any).
   - Whether the firm's research and information match your investing preferences.
   - The firm's track record for outages. This is still the Achilles' heel of the Internet. What methods does the firm use to shore up its reliability when on-line service is interrupted?

5. **Scrutinize service quality.** Before choosing any firm, be sure to investigate the level of customer service provided. Even if you want no help at all with your investment decisions, you still require a basic

level of customer support. Ask people who use the firm how satisfied they are in these areas:

- Hours of operation and telephone accessibility. An inexpensive brokerage that's not open when you want to make a trade is hardly a bargain. The same is true for telephone service—low trading fees aren't worth the risk of busy signals and lost opportunities to trade at the price you want.
- How swiftly trades are executed. Once you've put in your order, how fast can the firm come up with enough buyers or sellers?
- Real-time quotes. If you plan to do daily or rapid-fire trading, will this firm give the exact price of the stock at the moment you call (or log on)? What is the charge for this service?
- Easy-to-understand statements. Ask a prospective firm to send you a sample statement. You would be unhappy to find you need the Rosetta Stone to decipher the year-end account statement.

6. **Don't sacrifice stability.** Make sure any broker-age you sign with is insured by the government-sponsored Securities Investor Protection Corporation. Don't entrust your money to a trading firm without SIPC coverage.

7. **Ask about a minimum.** Some brokerage firms require a minimum investment to open an account. Determine how much money you want to invest, and find out if you're playing in the right league be-fore you launch into any other questions.

8. **Request an information packet.** Ask each prospective brokerage to send you a packet listing all their fees and charges. This is the only way to know if the rock-bottom commission fee that's ad-vertised is a true bargain, or only the tip of the fi-nancial iceberg.

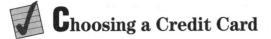

Choosing a Credit Card

Don't leave home with just any credit card. Most lending institutions will be only too happy to fill your wallet with plastic—no matter what your ability to pay or credit history may be. This checklist will assist you with your real challenge: to sort through the array of tempting offers and choose a card that best suits your financial situation.

1. **Consider the APR.** The APR, or annual percentage rate, is the actual cost of the card over the span of a year. It includes the interest rate, annual fee, and other service charges. Comparing APRs among cards is a quick way to see which may cost you less. But you'll need to weigh other factors in your decision.

2. **Decide how you'll pay off the card.** If you plan to carry a balance from month to month (not a great idea, by the way, because there are cheaper ways to finance purchases), choose a card with low interest rates. If you know you'll pay your balance in full each month, the interest rate is less relevant, and you can focus on other features a card might offer.

3. **Ask what your card can do for you.** Some cards give you a little something in return for your business. Many offer frequent-flyer miles for the money you spend. Some, like Discover Card and Ameritech Complete MasterCard, offer cash rebates. Others allow you to accumulate credits toward the purchase of a new car, or to support your favorite charity or your alma mater with each purchase. You're likely to pay a higher annual fee for these cards, so whether the benefits are worth the expense is a decision that only you can make.

4. **Look at annual fees.** These can run anywhere from $35 to $90 a year. If you plan to pay your balance in full each month, and aren't interested in frequent flyer miles or other extras, you should have no trouble finding a card with no annual fee. Occasionally, an annual fee may be waived for new customers or for longtime card holders. If you have an excellent credit history, or do significant business with the lender, it couldn't hurt to ask about a fee waiver.

5. **Search for grace.** Now here's a reason to read (or at least scan) the fine print. You're looking for the words "grace period," which translate as the number of days before a lender starts the interest meter ticking on your purchase. On a card with no grace period you'll owe interest from the day you make a purchase, even if you pay the bill promptly. Look for a card with a twenty-five-day grace period.

6. **What's your interest?** You'll sometimes have a choice between two types of interest rates: variable and fixed. Variable, or floating rates, tend to be lower than fixed; they're usually tied to the bank's prime rate or the recent cost of Treasury bills. As the name suggests, you can't know from month to month how much interest you'll be paying. Fixed rates aren't exactly carved in stone either. Banks change them every year or so at will, and with no warning.

7. **Beware of introductions.** Low introductory rates are a frequent credit card marketing device. These seductively low introductory rates eventually (and sometimes quickly) zoom upward, becoming anything but a bargain. If you do take advantage of such a rate, make sure the lender doesn't take advantage of you. Keep your eye on the expiration of the low rate and switch cards when the time comes.

8. **Watch for other fees.** Some card issuers charge a fee when you go over your credit limit. Some charge a late payment fee—in addition to the extra finance charges. And many lenders charge a transaction fee for cash advances on your card, over and above the interest rate for this quick and easy, but pricey loan.

9. **Less is more.** Contrary to what many people assume, the fewer credit cards you own, the more impressive your credit rating looks. Prospective lenders tend to interpret multiple credit cards as multiple opportunities to get into debt. Find one or two cards that work well with your spending and payment patterns and keep your credit file attractively slim.

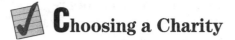 Choosing a Charity

The best-intentioned people sometimes shy from donating money to charities because they're uncertain
about which ones to support. Equally well-intentioned
people sometimes give more than is prudent—or
choose unworthy causes—for the same reason. Charitable giving should be approached the same way you
make other financial decisions. Here are some suggestions to keep in mind.

1. **Resist pressure.** Never give just because a solicitor
   makes you feel embarrassed or guilty. In fact, be suspicious of any charities that use high pressure or
   highly emotional appeals on prospective donors.

2. **Don't hand it over.** Avoid giving money during a
   face-to-face solicitation at your front door or in a
   public place. If you think the cause is worth sup-
   porting, request literature and give yourself time to
   check the organization's legitimacy and consider the
   amount you'll donate.

3. **Watch out for $20 candy bars.** Be very cautious
   about charities that telephone or come to your door
   asking you to purchase common items—from pencils or candy to household goods and first aid kits—
   at inflated prices.

4. **Go with those you know.** Choosing a cause
   you're familiar with helps you feel good about making the donation and also increases the likelihood
   that your money will be spent in the way you intend.

5. **Be alert to questionable charities.** Some
   "charities" are little more than operations with
   sound-alike names to help them skim away money

from legitimate causes. Don't assume a charity is worthy because its name sounds good. Get the exact name in writing before you contribute.

6. **Get a dollar breakdown.** Find out how much of every dollar you give is used for charitable purposes (as opposed to salaries and overhead). The National Charities Information Bureau's standards require that a minimum of sixty cents out of each dollar spent is dedicated to charitable use. NCIB and the Better Business Bureau publish reports evaluating individual charities. You can research the charity you're considering by going to either Web site (www.ncib.org and www.bbb.org).

7. **Stick to a budget.** Make your decisions about charitable giving at one time each year, deciding how much and where to donate your money. Planning ahead will enable you to achieve your philanthropic and tax goals and protect yourself from hasty decisions based on emotional appeals.

✓ End-of-the-Year Tax Strategies

Here are some smart tax-saving tips recommended by seasoned certified public accountant Sue Miller of McLean, Virginia. Following this list can help boost your deductions and defer as much end-of-the-year income as possible.

1. **Clean out and donate.** Organize your closet (see page 40) and donate clothes that no longer fit to your local charity. Box up old toys your children don't play with any more and donate them to a charity.

2. **Review your charitable contributions.** If the total is lower than you'd like, make more. Before the end of the year is a good time to do this because contributions are still tax deductible.

3. **Consider donating appreciated stock.** You can give stock to your favorite charity and take a deduction for the fair market value. This way, your out-of-pocket cost will only be what you originally paid for the stock.

4. **Consider taking stock losses.** Selling stocks that are losers can offset capital gains you may have realized during the year.

5. **Pay state tax early.** If you anticipate owing taxes, pay your state income tax on December 31, rather than waiting for the January 15 due date for the fourth-quarter estimated payment.

6. **Visit your dentist.** To obtain a deduction for medical expenses, your out-of-pocket medical expenses must exceed 7.5 percent of your adjusted gross income. If you are close to this amount, fit that extra orthodontist visit or that new pair of eyeglasses in before the end of the year.

7. **Pay your mortgage early.** Consider making your January mortgage payment in December. This will give you an extra interest deduction on your return.

8. **Delay invoicing.** If you are a cash-basis, self-employed taxpayer, delay sending out those December invoices to your customers to defer income into the following year.

9. **Consider retirement.** If you are self-employed, consider setting up a pension plan for your business. A Keogh must be set up by December 31. If you miss this deadline, a SEP can be set up by the due date of your tax return.

10. **Call your accountant.** Find out what's new in deductions for the year so you don't miss a chance to save money.

✔️ Frequently Overlooked Tax Deductions

You don't want to be rash when listing deductions on your annual income tax form. But neither do you want to overlook those to which you may be legally entitled. Check this list for any you might be neglecting to claim.

1. **Points.** A one-time mortgage-closing fee is expressed in "points," or a percentage of the mortgage charged by the lender for making a loan. (For example, a charge of three points on a $100,000 mortgage means the borrower pays $3,000.) The dollar amount of these points is deductible from your federal income tax the year that a loan is made for the purpose of buying a home, or a loan is taken out to pay for major remodeling on a principal residence. When a home is refinanced, the points paid are pro-rated over the life of the loan; they cannot be deducted all in one tax year.

2. **Publications related to tax and finance.** This includes books, magazines, and newsletters on financial or tax matters. You may also deduct money spent for daily publications such as *The Wall Street Journal, Investors Daily,* and *The New York Times.*

3. **Charitable service expenses.** When you donate your professional services or personal time to a tax-deductible charitable institution, you are entitled to deduct any out-of-pocket expenses you incur. You may also deduct per mile auto usage, parking, and tolls.

4. **Health insurance.** If you are self-employed—and *only* if you are self-employed—you may deduct a portion of the premium you pay for your own insurance.

5. **December deductibles.** Deductions can be taken on items you charged in December even if you don't pay for them until January of the new year (as long as they were deductible in the first place).

6. **Unreimbursed business expenses** are deductible when they exceed 2 percent of your adjusted taxable income. For example, if your taxable income is $100,000 and you spend $2,001 on business expenses for which you weren't compensated by your employer, the single dollar (the amount in excess of 2 percent of $100,000) would be deductible. For some taxpayers, they can add up fast. Some examples:
   - Use of your automobile and cost of local transportation for business purposes, exclusive of going to and from work.
   - Business use of home phone, cellular phone, and pay phone.
   - Stationery, office supplies, photocopies, etc., purchased for work.
   - Continuing education, including expenses related to seminars attended for business purposes, registration fees, travel, lodging, and 50 percent of the cost of meals.
   - Lodging and living expenses on a business trip, including valet services and tips to doormen, bellhops, etc.
   - Half the cost of food and drink when on a business trip.
   - Gifts to business associates (up to $25 per person per year).
   - Cost of sprucing up or decorating office, including fresh flowers.
   - Half the cost of entertaining business associates.
   - Half the cost of entertaining business associates at home when business is the primary purpose of the gathering.

7. **Personal property taxes on cars and trucks** when they are based on the fair market value of the vehicle.

8. **Additional amount of state taxes** you pay at the beginning of a new year for the previous tax year is deductible in the year paid.

TIPS ON KEEPING INCOME TAX RECORDS

- Keep anything related to your tax return, including receipts and canceled checks for deductible items, along with W-2 and 1099 forms for at least three years, the IRS's statute of limitations on auditing most returns. Just to be safe, however, hold on to records for at least six years; the IRS has that amount of time to audit anyone it suspects of underreporting income by 25 percent or more. There is no statute of limitations on fraud.

- Keep track of any money you spend on home improvements. This amount won't be deductible on your annual income taxes, but it can reduce the taxable gain when your home is sold.

- If you have a business at home, keep business expenses and records separate from personal expenses. If possible, have a credit card, checking account, and telephone line devoted exclusively to your business activities. If it isn't possible to do so, and you use some items (such as your car, telephone line, or computer) for both purposes, faithfully keep a log of these expenses. The IRS has a fairly keen sense for expense journals that have been composed hastily the night before an audit.

✔️ How to Buy Homeowner's Insurance

You absolutely, positively cannot do without home-owner's insurance if you own your own home. It covers you against most types of damage to your home and loss or theft of its contents. It also protects you financially if anyone is injured on your property. But how do you choose the right policy?

1. **Buy enough coverage.** All mortgage lenders require homeowner's coverage for at least the amount of the loan. But don't assume that's all you need. Your policy should cover 80 to 85 percent of the cost to rebuild or replace your home from the foundation up—which will be more than your mortgage or the resale value of your home. Ask your insurer or check with a contractor or professional appraiser to determine this amount.

2. **Balance risks and coverage cost.** Standard policies do not cover earthquakes and floods. If you live in an area prone to either, look into the cost of adding this coverage. But be prepared to forgo it if the price of the policy and the size of the deductible make this coverage too expensive.

3. **Know what you're not getting.** Depending on the type of policy you choose, you will usually be covered for about a dozen risks, including fire and theft. But if you want broader coverage in case of damage due to burst pipes or defective wiring, you may need to spend more.

4. **Find out how the policy figures losses.** *Actual cash value* may sound good, but it means, for example, that you'd receive replacement cost of your household goods—minus the value they've lost over the years you've owned them (depreciation). Loss of

a television set you bought for $600 five years ago might bring you half the amount you paid—not quite enough to purchase the same item today. *Replacement coverage,* on the other hand, gives you the money you'd need to go out today and replace the items you lost, regardless of their value after depreciation. Replacement coverage typically costs 10 or 15 percent more than actual cash value, but you can offset the higher premium by taking a higher deductible.

5. **Consider special coverage.** Standard policies limit coverage on certain rare or expensive personal belongings like antiques, jewelry, furs, and art. If you own any of these, talk to your agent about a separate policy (known as a floater) or an addition to your current policy (an endorsement or rider) to cover them specifically.

6. **Reduce your premium.** Ask your insurance agent about discounts for homeowners who install deadbolt locks, smoke alarms, fire extinguishers, and security systems. You can also opt for a higher deductible (the amount out of your pocket before the insurance company pays on a claim) to reduce the premium. You may also be eligible for lower premiums by purchasing all your insurance policies (auto, homeowners, etc.) from the same company.

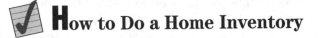

How to Do a Home Inventory

No matter how carefully you select your homeowner's insurance policy, you can't collect money for items you fail to report stolen or damaged because you forgot about them. Taking a home inventory may not be the most enjoyable way to spend a day, but it's the only sure way to know what you've got and to protect it.

1. **Photograph everything.** Use a video or still camera to document your belongings. If you use a video camera, talk about each item as you go.
   - Shoot an overview of each room to show what's in it.
   - Open every closet, cabinet, drawer, and cupboard and shoot close enough to show contents.
   - Don't forget to photograph clothing and shoes, taking note of especially costly items.
   - Take close-ups of small valuable items to show detail.
   - Don't forget to inventory attics, cellars, storerooms, and laundry hampers.

2. **Make a descriptive list.** Pictures alone aren't enough. Write a description of each item and include serial numbers and brand names.

3. **Save receipts** for every item of value you purchase. Circle the price and date of purchase and keep the receipts with the inventory.

4. **Have special items appraised.** Antiques, oriental rugs, art, stamp or coin collections, silverware, jewelry, furs, and other valuables should be appraised and carefully described. Photograph them so it's clear they're in your home (not at an antique store or in a museum!).

5. **Don't overlook the humble items.** It's not necessary to write elaborate descriptions of each article you own, but if you lost everything, you'd want help remembering the cookie sheets, clocks, bookends, houseplants, and dog bed.

6. **Go outside.** Don't neglect outdoor improvements like decks and landscaping and items such as tool sheds, patio furniture, and gardening tools.

7. **Include seasonal items.** If you make the inventory in the spring, search out your winter supplies and record snow shovels, snow blowers, winter clothing, and so forth.

8. **Keep the inventory safe.** Now that you've gone to all this trouble, put copies of the inventory where they'll be protected in the event of a fire or other calamity at your home. One copy with receipts, appraisals, descriptions, and photos should go in your safe deposit box. You might want to leave another copy with a close friend or relative, or ask your insurance agent if he'd be willing to store one for you.

9. **Keep inventory current.** Whenever you purchase something new, clip the receipt to a photo and description of the item, and add these to the inventory in your safe deposit box the next time you're at the bank.

Tip One way to ease the burden of creating a home inventory is to make it a household project. If your children are old enough, consider assigning different rooms to each family member. Load up on disposable cameras, pads, and pens for everyone.

Professional Life

Every businessperson, including veteran professionals, confronts situations where they'd appreciate a little advice. Lists can pare down even the most intimidating or abstract business project into one that seems manageable. Success is sure to follow, one checkmark at a time!

✓ Ten Tips for Effective Networking

Networking is one of those business buzzwords that makes many people cringe. But networking is not about shoving your business card into the hands of strangers while boasting about yourself! Self-promotion specialist Ilise Benun defines networking as talking about your work to people who want to listen and helping them get to know you and what you have to offer. "People want to work with people they trust," says Benun, "but how will anyone work with you if they don't know you're there? And if you don't tell them, who will?" Here are some tips for networking effectively—without making anyone uncomfortable.

1. **Join professional organizations and get busy.** Just joining an organization isn't enough; you need to get to know people on a personal level

and allow them to see you in action. Volunteer for a
working committee, take minutes, organize events,
or get involved in any way that makes a contribution and helps you become visible in the organization.

2. **Sharpen your "elevator speech."** Be able to explain what you do in the time it takes an elevator to
go a few floors—fifteen to twenty seconds at most.
Don't think of it as a sales pitch, just as an intrigu-
ing way to introduce yourself professionally.

3. **Be a card carrier.** You'll defeat your purpose if
you arrive at a meeting or event without a stack of
your business cards. And you never know when you
might run into someone at the grocery store who
provides a perfect networking opportunity.

4. **Get the card thing over with.** Exchanging
cards is "a crucial part of the ritual," according to
Benun, who admits it can be awkward. Her advice is
to plunge right in and say something like, "Hey, let's
get the business card thing out of the way." Done!
And no one feels embarrassed.

5. **Make one friend.** You won't make a friend the
first time you meet someone, of course. But if you
can find at least one person you can talk with when
you attend an event, the occasion will seem less intimidating. And you never know how many people
you may wind up talking to just because you sought
out one person.

6. **It's not about you.** The people you meet in most
settings, professional and social, are usually thinking about themselves; it's a trait most humans share.
Shifting your attention from yourself to the concerns of your networking prospects will make you
stand out. When you've asked good questions and
paid attention to the answers, you will become

someone people are very interested in paying attention to.

7. **Go where they go.** Find out which events, conferences, meetings your prospects attend. You'll not only meet the people you're interested in, you'll learn something new about their interests and concerns.

8. **Look for low-key opportunities.** Don't overlook the networking possibilities inherent in your beach volleyball games, book group meetings, church gatherings, or any of your other nonprofessional encounters. Sometimes the best contacts are made when no one is thinking about business and conversation evolves more naturally.

9. **What's new with me?** A few times a week, ask yourself what is new and interesting in your life and business: What projects are you working on? What are you trying to accomplish in the short/long run? Any creative problems you'd like to discuss? Whenever you run into someone you haven't seen in a while, you'll be prepared to make the most of your encounter.

10. **Follow up.** No matter how many business cards you hand out and take in, you won't have achieved much unless you get in touch afterward. Benun suggests establishing a follow-up procedure that's easy and fast. It could be as simple as keeping a stack of stamped postcards handy for sending a note, or setting aside time every week to stick a Post-It note on your brochure and mail it to new acquaintances.

The Perfect Presentation: How to Prepare

Many people would rather face a firing squad than an audience. In fact, studies consistently show that public speaking is the number one fear for most people, while dying falls well behind at number six. Take a deep breath and follow these pointers to ensure that you do the best possible job the next time you make a presentation.

1. **Practice makes perfect.** Remember the old joke about how to get to Carnegie Hall: "Practice, practice, practice!" Practice your talk so thoroughly that you know your stuff cold. Knowing you are as prepared as possible will bolster your confidence. Record your speech once or twice and play it back; you'll know what you need to work on. Feeling confident about your delivery will ease stage fright.

2. **Don't write out the whole talk.** Use only key words to jog your memory as you speak. Make sure you've got all your pages or index cards—and that they are in the right order!

3. **Get to the room early** to ensure that:
   - The mike works and is adjusted for your height.
   - The lighting is adequate.
   - There is water at the lectern.
   - The audiovisual equipment is working.

4. **Check the mirror:**
   - Is your fly zipped?
   - Is your lipstick neatly applied?
   - Are your teeth free of food?
   - Is your slip out of sight?
   - Is your hair combed?
   - Are the bottoms of your shoes free of toilet paper or other trailing debris?

5. **Prepare your introducer.** He should have background material to work with and should know how to pronounce your name correctly.

6. **Give some thought to reasonable replies** for possible hostile or tough questions.

7. **Put your watch on the podium** in front of you so you can keep track of the time.

8. **Stand up straight.**

9. **Speak slowly.** Most people have a tendency to speak too quickly when they're onstage, so if you slow yourself down deliberately, you'll probably be at about the right pace.

10. **Don't be afraid to pause** if you need to collect your thoughts or if you lose your place in your talk. A moment's quiet may seem like hours to you, but the audience will hardly notice. A dignified pause is much better than rambling or saying "um" to fill the silence.

11. **If your hands shake**—and adrenaline can do this to you even if you're not feeling nervous—steady them on the podium instead of holding on to rattling papers. You'll feel calmer knowing no one can see your nerves.

12. **Remember that even if the worst happens,** you'll live to laugh about it.

Tip You'd be better off not asking any family or friends to lend moral support at your next talk, according to a recent study published in the *Journal of Personality and Social Psychology*. Research shows that people facing a hostile audience tend to perform much better because they feel they have nothing to lose. Those familiar faces can actually cramp your style because you have more at stake.

CONTROLLING STAGE FRIGHT Consider the physical agonies many people endure when faced with a roomful of people waiting to hear them speak. Sweating, shaking, nausea, pounding heart, quavering voice, and difficulty breathing won't kill you, but they certainly undermine confidence! Here are the steps most frequently recommended by psychologists and performance coaches for controlling that fear.

- **As you wait to go onstage,** remember that the worst will be behind you the moment you reach the podium. Stage fright is usually at its worst right before the performance.
- **Focus on the goal of your talk** (to inform, entertain, motivate, or persuade). Make achieving the goal more interesting to yourself than feeling the anxiety.
- **Take plenty of deep breaths.** You can literally make yourself sick with shallow, nervous breathing. Breathing deeply will help ease your physical symptoms and restore your poise.
- **Envision your audience as a group of friendly people.** In fact, they probably are pulling for you. Most audiences want to like the speaker just as much as the speaker wants to be liked.
- **Keep in mind that you always appear more confident** than you feel. Those butterflies in your stomach may feel real, but no one can see them!
- **Ask your doctor** about the medications known as beta blockers. They aren't tranquilizers and don't affect your alertness or alter your mental state, but they do block the adrenaline rush that leads to stage fright symptoms. Beta blockers are prescription drugs (and should never be taken by anyone with asthma), so talk with your doctor if nothing else has worked for you.

Smart Strategies for Business Trips

Even seasoned business travelers can overlook crucial details—those that can make all the difference in on-the-road productivity—when packing for a last-minute trip. Use this checklist to make yourself a savvy business traveler.

 ## To Bring

1. **Must-have telephone numbers.** Unless you're lucky enough to have an electronic organizer, chances are you don't carry your Rolodex in your briefcase. Take time to copy down all the phone numbers and addresses you'll need before you leave home. (Save time by getting directions to your destination before you arrive.)

2. **Full set of local clients' phone numbers.** Don't limit your "traveling Rolodex" to the clients or associates you're scheduled to meet. You never know when your plans might change or an urgent matter necessitating an unscheduled visit might come up.

3. **Emergency cash or bankcard.** Finding out you have no cash as you leave your bags with the porter or hail a taxi can be extremely inconvenient. Consider keeping an emergency stash securely locked in your briefcase, or at least an "emergency twenty" in your wallet. A bankcard is the next best thing—stop by an airport ATM before your first meeting.

4. **A list of restaurants and bars in town.** Prepare yourself with a list of recommended spots so you can confidently take a client to lunch without asking for suggestions. The list will also be handy if you need to spend a quiet half hour between appointments.

To Do

1. **Know how to access your messages.** Make sure you know the phone numbers and codes required for remote access of your phone messages. If you have a secretary, rather than a voice-mail system, be sure you know her number—you may not call it much under ordinary circumstances.

2. **Keep your laptop close.** Many a laptop has been pinched while its owner talks on the telephone or pays for coffee. If you must put your laptop down in a public place, secure the strap by wrapping it once around your wrist or leg.

3. **Be discreet.** Be careful of conversations on the airplane, in the airport lounge, or in any public place. You never know when your remarks are being overheard.

Your Computer

Most of us work with computers every day, but this constant exposure doesn't necessarily make us feel confident about using them. If you're bewildered by mentions of megabytes, puzzled by debates over system upgrades, and intimidated by technology in general, you're in good company. But even the world of technology can be tamed with a few checklists. Once you know what to do and what to ask, you can find a computer that works just right for you —and keep it working that way.

 Computer Shopping Tips

Shopping for a computer is a little like ordering food in a foreign country: you may have a general idea of what you want, but you aren't sure how to ask for it. Because innovations occur so rapidly, no book can give specifics about which machines to consider. But these shopping tips will offer good basic advice even as technology changes.

1. **Determine your needs.** Computers are not "one-size-fits-all" technology. Before you decide what to purchase, evaluate how you will be using your com-

puter: writing letters, keeping financial records, playing games, tutoring your children, sending and receiving e-mail, and so forth. If you plan to bring work home from the office, make sure you have software that can run your office files, or that you have the ability to connect remotely to your office network. If you have a computer gamer in your house, you might need speakers, video, and multimedia capability to make the computer games soar. Plan on building your own Web site? You'll need a system that's Internet friendly.

2. **Do your homework.** You may be surprised how interesting computer magazines become when you're thinking of buying a new computer. Scoop up a handful at a local newsstand (a few to look for: *PC Magazine, PC World, Mac World, Home Office Computing, Small Business Computing*). Read the computer column in your local newspaper. Familiarize yourself with what's available in the way of features (see "Computer Lingo," p. 265).

3. **Create your budget.** The computer itself is only part of your purchase. If you fail to budget for the various add-ons (sometimes called peripherals), you will find yourself with either a system that disappoints you or a bill that surprises you. Some of the items you will want to include in your budget:
   - Computer
   - Monitor
   - Printer
   - Software
   - Keyboard and mouse or trackball
   - Drive for backing up your data (like a tape drive or Zip)
   - Additional memory
   - Modem
   - Speakers

- Power protection
- Scanner or digital camera
- Internet connection

4. **Get the most computer you can for your budget.** Computer technology changes quickly, but the amount you will need to spend to get an adequate computer system remains fairly constant. Instead of setting your sights on a specific computer and waiting for the price to hit your budget, set your budget first, then get the fastest computer you can for your money.

5. **Macintosh or Windows?** There's little difference in price between these two computing platforms, and most common computer applications, like word processing, personal finance, and Internet software, are readily available for both. Conventional wisdom is that Macs are easier to set up and use and are tops in graphics. Windows PCs, on the other hand, dominate the market and have a broader software selection. Make your decision based on what you're most comfortable with; whether you need a computer that's compatible with what you have at the office; and what software you need to use.

6. **Desktop or laptop?** If you plan to take your computer on the road, or if desk space is extremely limited, consider using a laptop (or notebook) as your primary computer. But be warned that portables are just as powerful as their desktop counterparts, but they are more expensive and less expandable. Laptops also have smaller screens that can be harder to read, and smaller keyboards that are not as responsive. If you do decide to buy a laptop, you might want to consider combining it with a docking station—an attachment that lets you add a full-size monitor and keyboard.

7. **Buy from the right source.** There are a plethora of places you can buy a computer—your local computer store, a computer superstore, a consumer electronics store, an office supply store, or mail order. Buy from a place where you feel comfortable. Make sure the salesperson takes the time to explain everything to you so you understand it. Ask about service and support options: Will the store help you set up the computer? What will they do if it doesn't work? What is the return policy? You might want to consider paying extra for additional support just for peace of mind. If you don't need much hand holding, you might want to consider mail order, which can be less expensive and highly reliable. If you do buy mail order, pay by credit card so you have recourse if you run into problems.

8. **Choose a brand name.** If you're new to computers, stick with a name you know. A "house" brand or a computer built by your cousin might be cheaper, but you could find yourself in a pickle should it suddenly start to malfunction.

9. **Don't forget about training.** If you're a novice, be sure to sign up for some computer classes. The money invested will pay off in the long run in a more compelling computer experience.

10. **Look for bundles.** Many computer stores now sell "bundled" systems that contain all the hardware and software you need. These can make shopping easier and save you money. Be sure to buy the right bundle—a "family" package that contains home entertainment and educational software won't do the trick if you plan to use your computer to run a home-based business.

Computer Lingo

Like any foreign territory, the world of computers has its own language. Master a few key terms and you'll find the natives much friendlier.

1. **Processor.** The processor chip is the "brain" of your computer. Windows computers use Intel chips like the Pentium, or Intel clones like those made by AMD or Cyrix. Macintosh computers use a processor called the PowerPC. Processors are rated by speed, which is measured in megahertz (MHz)—this is like the horsepower rating of a car engine.

2. **Operating system.** This is the software that tells your computer how to work. Windows is the operating system for most computers. Macintosh computers use their own, separate operating system. The operating system comes with your computer.

3. **Memory (RAM).** The amount of memory, or RAM (random access memory), affects how quickly your computer works with your software. For most users, the amount of RAM you have will have more of an effect on your computer's performance than will your processor speed.

4. **Hard disk drive.** Think of your hard drive as your computer's filing cabinet. It stores all the software and data. Hard drive capacity is measured in gigabytes (GB) or billions of bytes.

5. **Floppy disk.** This is the little 3 ½-inch square disk that slips into the front of some computers. Floppies used to be the primary way software was loaded into your computer, or data was taken out of your computer. That's no longer the case—most software now comes on CD-ROMs.

6. **CD-ROM drive.** A CD-ROM drive operates a disk that looks just like the one that goes in your home CD player, but it holds software instead of music. Most software today comes packaged on CD-ROMs, which hold much more data than floppies. CD-ROM drives are rated in terms of how fast they retrieve the information from the disk: a 32x drive does it 32 times faster than an original 1x drive.

7. **Modem.** The modem (which, if you're interested, stands for "modulator/demodulator") is what allows your computer to communicate with the Internet over your phone line. The faster your modem is, the faster your computer will be able to load and send information through the Internet.

8. **Monitor.** This is the computer display screen. Like televisions, monitors are sized by measuring diagonally from the top corner to the opposite bottom corner. The screen's resolution is measured in pixels, and sharpness is measured by "dot pitch" in millimeters.

9. **Video RAM (VRAM).** This is specialized memory that lets your video monitor work with your computer. The more VRAM you have, the faster your graphics will load and run. This is especially important for multimedia software like games and certain Internet applications.

10. **Keyboard and mouse.** Your computer comes with a keyboard and mouse, but make sure they're ones you feel comfortable with. The keyboard should have some cushioning to reduce the impact on your fingers, wrists, and body. A mouse should feel responsive. Watch out for flimsy keyboards and mice—you'll end up paying for them with aching fingers and wrists.

11. **Software.** Software is what lets your computer accomplish certain tasks. You need different software

packages to do word processing, use the Internet, or keep track of your household finances. Most computers now come with many of these software "applications." Some basic software to look for:

- An office suite that contains a word processor, spreadsheet, and database.
- A Web browser for accessing the Internet and sending and receiving e-mail.
- Personal finance software for keeping your household accounts.
- Virus protection to protect your computer from assorted mischief makers.

BUYING FOR THE FUTURE To make sure the computer you buy today is the computer you'll be happy with a year from now, keep these ideas in mind as you shop:

- When choosing a monitor, look for one with a resolution of 768×1024. Sharpness is measured by "dot pitch" in millimeters—smaller is better. Most PC users will want a dot pitch of .28 or lower.
- Double your RAM, and you'll extend the useful life of your computer significantly. In general, computers tend to come with the minimum amount of RAM necessary to run the latest software. But newer, more sophisticated software, requiring ever more RAM, comes along all the time. If you buy twice the RAM your computer comes with at the time you make the purchase, you won't have to upgrade RAM when you want to run the newest applications.
- Don't get carried away with elaborate software packages you may never use. You will need different software to do word processing, use the Internet, or keep track of your household finances; but evaluate the package based on your current needs. Unlike RAM, software is easy to add later.

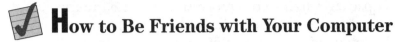

How to Be Friends with Your Computer

This ten-point checklist tells you what you need to know and what you must do to coexist peacefully and productively with that inscrutable constant companion, your computer.

1. **Make backups.** Any data that you create yourself is vulnerable to disasters, from power surges and viruses to equipment failure and human error. But the best disaster insurance in the world is free: Back up everything you create onto a diskette, so you will have a copy of your work separate from your hard drive. Save your work every fifteen minutes or so and save it onto a diskette at the same time. The process only takes a few seconds, and the habit could save you hours or weeks of time and grief.

2. **If it works, don't upgrade it.** As the old saying goes: If it ain't broke, don't fix it. If Windows 95 is doing a good job for you, don't rush out to get Windows 98 just because it's there. Any time you change operating systems, you risk losing data and you're more prone to battling bugs that haven't been worked out by the manufacturer. Don't be Bill Gates's free beta tester.

3. **Upgrade with more RAM.** You need a minimum of 32 MG of RAM (random access memory) to efficiently run many of today's programs. You'll get more for your money by upgrading the amount of RAM on your computer instead of buying a whole new computer. There is, however, one major caveat: don't upgrade a platform less than a 586 (Pentium). For example, if you're starting with a 486, first spend your money for the more advanced platform, then upgrade further by increasing its work capacity with more RAM.

4. **Buy a second hard drive instead of replacing a small with a larger one.** When you add a second hard drive you save yourself the trouble of transferring data to a new one. And when you think of all the bookmarks, e-mail addresses, and programs you use, you begin to realize just what a blessing that can be.

5. **Buy antivirus software and keep current with the updates.** See "Protecting Your Computer from Viruses" on page 273.

6. **Beware of strangers.** Always download files to a floppy disk and run your virus check software before you open a file or execute a program from an unknown source. Remember that you can only get a virus from opening a program on your hard drive.

7. **Buy a good surge protector.** Avoid the inexpensive ones (around $10) which use a metal oxide varistor (MOV) suppression system that can fail in areas with frequent surges. Especially if you live in an area with frequent surges, spend about $100 to get one that won't fail.

8. **Keep at least 100 MB free on your hard drive.** Today's software uses part of the hard drive in addition to RAM. If you don't have enough room on your hard drive, your applications won't run smoothly. To check your hard drive in Windows 95, open Explore and select the Hard Drive window; that will tell you how much space is free. In DOS, type CHKDSK, then hit enter and it will give you the information.

9. **Purchase the right modem.** Don't believe everything you hear about the value of 56K modems. By federal law, you can't get anything faster than 53K and in reality you'll be lucky to get 44K. To work efficiently on-line and send and receive files and e-

mail, you need a minimum of 28K. The old 1440 speed is completely inadequate for today's technology.

10. **Keep all documentation that comes with your system** and any software you purchase separately. This will help with resale, upgrades, and calling the company in the event you need technical assistance.

✔ E-mail Etiquette

E-mail has created a new frontier in communication.
It's faster and cheaper than sending paper-and-stamp
letters, and the sheer ease of sending of e-mail encour-
ages a certain informality. It's now possible to dash off a
note to pretty much anyone we choose—from the president of the company to your long-lost cousin Betty.
This opens up exciting new territory, but it's wise to
learn a few rules of the road before rushing in.

1. **Don't shout.** Typing with ALL CAPS in e-mail is
   the electronic equivalent of shouting and is considered bad manners.

2. **Be brief.** Keep your e-mail as brief as possible. Your
   message will be clear—and more welcome—if you
   say what you mean in the fewest possible words.
   Lengthy messages that flow through screen after
   screen are less likely to be read by busy people.

3. **Write clear headlines.** The subject line of an e-
   mail form is intended to let the recipient know at a
   glance what the e-mail is about. Subject lines such
   as "a question" or "hi" are unhelpful and can be
   downright annoying to those who prefer to sort and
   prioritize e-mails before opening them. A descriptive
   subject line is a big help to the reader.

4. **Cool off.** Never give in to the temptation to fire off
   an angry or sarcastic message. A tap of the "send"
   button makes this easy to do, but making amends
   afterward may be more difficult. Use your "save
   draft" file to hold messages until you are calm
   enough to reread before sending.

5. **Forward selectively.** A joke that's new and hilari-
   ous to you might not be to someone who's already

seen it or to someone who's so busy that extra e-mail is a nuisance. Don't get in the habit of routinely forwarding jokes and various other e-mails to everyone on your address list; send them only to those you're certain will appreciate receiving them.

6. **Reply sparingly.** Not every e-mail requires a reply and some need only a word or two. If you want to let the sender know you received something, a brief "Got it, thanks" is perfectly fine.

7. **Use good judgment.** If you're writing messages at work, be careful. Company e-mail can be retrieved and read and should not be considered private.

Protecting Your Computer from Viruses

A computer virus is a software program that gets into your computer like a germ and infects your system. The most innocuous viruses may set off a few noises or some pop-up graphics, but the most serious can cripple your computer and erase your data. If you use a computer, chances are pretty good that you will encounter a virus at some point. You can limit its impact by following these basic guidelines.

1. **Get your shots.** The only way to inoculate your computer is to install and use an antivirus software program. The most popular are Norton Anti-Virus (Symantec), VirusScan (McAfee/Network Associates), and Dr. Solomon's Anti-Virus or Virex (Dr. Solomon's/ Network Associates). All do essentially the same thing: they scan disks or data for known viruses and then eradicate any they find. This software is easy to set up and use. Configure it to scan a disk automatically when you insert it in your machine and to scan your hard drive each time you start up the computer for extra safety.

2. **Don't forget your boosters.** Something like six new computer viruses are discovered every day. Merely installing antivirus software won't do the trick. It is necessary to update your software frequently—every couple of months at least—to scan for these newly detected viruses. The major virus protection software publishers make these updates available for free from their websites. Remember to scan your disk for these new viruses every time you update.

3. **Never download from people you don't know.** This should be second nature, much like

looking both ways before crossing the street and not talking to strangers. People who write and spread viruses are sly—they try to disguise them in ways that catch you unaware so you'll slip an infected disk into your computer or download an e-mail attachment. Be very wary of offers like "free software!" that sound too good to be true. Be skeptical about e-mail that contains attachments you didn't request.

4. **Scan every disk you put in your computer.** Even shrink-wrapped software has the potential to contain a virus. Also, close the little plastic window in the top right corner of any disk before scanning it. This will "write-protect" the disk, meaning that your computer can read the disk but cannot write to it, thus keeping a virus from spreading.

5. **Back up your data.** Should a virus strike your computer, you will want to have a complete backup of your data and software to help you reconstitute your files. Copy all your files from your hard drive to a tape drive, Jazz or Zip disk, or other high-capacity removable drive. (Don't even consider floppies anymore for this purpose; they don't hold enough data.) Make these backups frequently—weekly if you use your computer daily. Another word of warning: if you've contracted a computer virus, be sure to scan and disinfect any recent backup files too. Otherwise, you risk reinfection.

6. **Don't panic.** If you do get a virus, don't worry. First, run a clean copy of your virus protection software to identify and remove the virus. In most cases, following the software's instructions will get you back up and running with no difficulties. If, however, you do experience problems, avoid drastic measures like reformatting your hard drive. Instead, contact your local computer professional for help.

Most data can be recovered from even the most infected machine.

7. **Watch out for virus hoaxes.** While there are thousands of genuine viruses, there are also some that only exist in people's imaginations. You may receive an e-mail informing you of a new virus and asking you to forward the message to everyone you know. Experts recommend that you ignore these messages, which are almost always hoaxes, and do not pass them on.

8. **Ask the experts.** Virus-tracking websites like Symantec's Anti-Virus Research Center post information on viruses, including what's real and what's not. Look at one of these sites before you panic. See the "Resources" section for a list of URLs.

Your Car

Most people depend on their car every day, whether they love cars and everything to do with them or remain as blissfully ignorant as possible. Beware: ignorance can be anything but blissful when it comes to keeping yourself safe in a well-maintained car. Here's the least you need to know.

What to Carry in Your Car

You never know when you might have a flat tire, a mechanical breakdown, or another roadside emergency. Thinking about emergencies ahead of time makes them much easier to deal with when they occur. Stock your car with the items on this checklist and you'll be prepared to handle whatever comes along.

1. **Cellular telephone.** No longer a luxury item reserved for the tycoon set, a cell phone can be as important as a spare tire when you travel by car. Check with AAA for details about their inexpensive emergency cell phone service.

2. **Proof of insurance,** even if your state doesn't require it.

3. **Automobile registration papers.**

4. **An accident report guide.** You can usually get one of these brief and simple guides from your insurance company or from AAA if you're a member. They make it much easier to gather complete information at the scene, and are especially helpful if you're feeling dazed or confused.

5. **Warning devices** such as flares and matches or reflective triangles.

6. **Jumper cables** with fully insulated handles.

7. **A first aid kit** plus any vital prescription medicines (see page 24).

8. **Flashlight with extra batteries.**

9. **Water.** Carry least a quart each for you and your car.

10. **Quick-energy "power" bars,** or other packaged food in case you're stranded. (If you tend to skip meals when in a hurry, these can make a big difference, too. You'll never get stuck with a growling stomach between errands again!)

11. **Paper towels and window cleaning fluid.** Driving at night with a smeared windshield (inside or out) can be extremely hazardous.

12. **Fire extinguisher.** Read the directions so you know how to use it quickly.

13. **Fully inflated spare tire.** Check it at least every few months.

14. **Portable tire pump,** plus a jack, lug wrench, and block of wood for emergency changes by the side of the road (when you'll be glad you have those flares).

15. **Aerosol flat fixer.** These can be great quick fixes for certain kinds of tire damage.

16. **Empty gas can.**

17. **Tool kit.** Carry a small standard toolkit or at least an adjustable wrench, large and small screwdrivers, and pliers.

18. **To be ultraprepared,** carry an inexpensive instant-picture camera to take "eyewitness" photos in case of an accident. As an alternative, you might keep a disposable camera in the car. However, without immediate results, you won't know in time if the picture turns out badly.

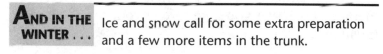

AND IN THE WINTER . . . Ice and snow call for some extra preparation and a few more items in the trunk.

- Heavy gloves and socks.
- Blanket.
- Cat litter, sand, or traction mats.
- Ice scraper and snow brush.
- A small snow shovel.
- Extra antifreeze.

 **C**ar Maintenance Checklist

Your owner's manual is the best and most authoritative guide to maintaining your car; different makes and models require specific services at varying intervals. Reading the manual will ensure that you keep up with vital maintenance and also help prevent your being "taken" by mechanics who might try to sell you services you don't actually need. If you don't have an owner's manual, this checklist can be your guide to the essential maintenance every vehicle must receive. Remember, the better you take care of your car, the better it will take care of you.

1. **Oil.** Check the level every week or so and change the oil and filter about every 3,000 miles.

2. **Fluids.** Check levels every six months, or before you go on long trips: battery fluid, brake and power steering fluid, transmission fluid and coolant (with antifreeze mixture in winter).

3. **Battery.** Check to see if the battery terminals and cables need cleaning whenever you have the oil changed.

4. **Tires.** Check your tire pressure at least once a month and inspect the tires for cuts and signs of uneven wear.

5. **Belts.** Check drive belts when the oil is changed. You can do this yourself by pushing down on the middle of each belt; if you can push down more than half an inch, the belt should be tightened.

6. **Change the air filter.** This should be done about every 15,000 miles or so.

7. **Safety checks.** Whether or not your state requires an annual safety inspection, it's a good idea to do a periodic check on the following:

- **Head- and taillights.** Get out of your car every now and then to see if all your lights work. Also check the headlight aim.
- **Horn.** Make sure it honks!
- **Brakes.** Check power brakes while the engine is running but the car is sitting still. Push the brake pedal down firmly and hold it; it should stop midway to the floor and stay there. If brakes feel "mushy," or if pedal keeps moving toward the floor, have your brakes checked right away.
- **Spare tire.** Take the spare out every couple of months to see that it's properly inflated.
- **Windshield wipers.** Turn them on regularly when it isn't raining and use your washer fluid to see how well the wipers clear it away. Make sure the washer fluid reservoir has plenty of fluid in it.

✓ How to Find a Good Mechanic

A good mechanic does much more than repair broken cars. You should also expect this person to charge fair prices, have your car ready when promised, stay up-to-date on automotive technology, and discuss your vehicle's problems in terms you can understand. Any mechanic who can't meet these standards doesn't deserve your business. The suggestions on this checklist will help you find a mechanic who does.

1. **Start now.** Look for a mechanic you can trust *before* you need one. Not only will you have the time to do a thorough search, you'll also have an opportunity to build at least name and face recognition at the repair shop. This can be reassuring if you need major repairs in an emergency.

2. **Talk to friends about repair shops they've used.** But don't accept a recommendation uncritically. Quiz your friends about how well their mechanic demonstrates the qualities of competence, good communication, reliability, and honesty.

3. **Look for ASE-certified mechanics.** Certification by the National Institute for Automotive Service Excellence doesn't guarantee honesty or even competence in all areas of auto mechanics. But ASE certification tests are difficult enough to weed out the mediocre or marginally competent. Because this certification is strictly voluntary, it's fair to assume that the shops who have it are concerned about the level of service they offer.

4. **Look on the walls of the office or waiting room** for other training certificates. A top-notch mechanic will take at least a couple of classes every year just to keep up with the latest technology. Ask

what schools or classes the shop owner or his employees regularly attend.

5. **Check both competence and honesty** by asking what the shop does when a vehicle that isn't working properly tests okay on all their equipment. The right answer to this question, according to automotive expert Mark Eskeldson, is for the mechanic to acknowledge that he's run into that situation. He should say that he researches the answer by consulting the several hundred pages of technical service bulletins published every year by the various automobile manufacturers. Consulting these bulletins (which can be kept at the station, accessed on-line, or on CD-ROM) is the only way to figure out some of the riddles posed by today's sophisticated automobile technology. Eskeldson advises you to be wary of a mechanic who claims he's never had such a problem. Your best bet: walk right out of the shop.

6. **Ask what brands of replacement parts the shop uses.** If you don't recognize any of the names, call an auto parts store and ask if those manufacturers make high-quality parts.

7. **Never choose a repair shop because it promises low prices.** The owner may dishonestly underestimate the cost of repairs, or may honestly be able to do the repairs cheaply because he hires untrained workers and uses cheap parts. Not much of a bargain in the long run.

8. **Beware of shops that offer both diagnosis and repair.** The shop that does both has a vested interest in finding something to repair. Take your car to an Automobile Association of America (or any other independent) diagnostic shop for an annual checkup. That list of needed (or soon to be needed)

repairs will make you a much smarter shopper when you look for a good mechanic.

9. **If your car breaks down on the road** don't let a tow truck driver talk you into towing your car to his "favorite" mechanic instead of your own. Even if you know that your mechanic doesn't handle the exact repair you'll need, you'll be better off getting a garage recommendation from someone you know and trust.

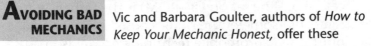

AVOIDING BAD MECHANICS   Vic and Barbara Goulter, authors of *How to Keep Your Mechanic Honest,* offer these three tips to the wise:

- Incompetent mechanics are most likely to be found at big chains where the pay is low.
- Dishonest mechanics are more likely to be met on the road, where they never expect to see their customers again.
- The best defense against dishonesty and trickery is watchfulness—keep an eye on your car when it's being serviced at an unfamiliar station.

✓ **W**hat to Do in an Accident

Even fender benders can be upsetting and affect our ability to think clearly. Consider keeping a copy of this checklist in your glove compartment so you can follow it if you are involved in any kind of accident.

1. **Pull off the road.** Do this as soon as it is safe and put on your emergency flashers. If you can't pull off, turn on your emergency flashers.

2. **Check for injuries.** Check yourself first, then see if anyone else is injured. Call 911 for paramedics, if needed.

3. **Call police.** Even in a minor accident, if property has been damaged, you may need a police report to file an insurance claim.

4. **Exchange information.** As you collect this information, give the other driver the same details about yourself:
   - Name, address, and phone number of the other driver. Take down work as well as home phone.
   - License plate number *and* driver's license number.
   - Insurance company's name, address, and the policy number (ask to see the card to verify this information).
   - Make, model, year, and color of the other car.
   - Names, addresses, and phone numbers of other passengers.

5. **Look for witnesses.** Ask for their names and home and work phone numbers.

6. **Get copy of police report.** If police do come to the scene and write up an accident report, ask for a copy of it. Also write down names and badge numbers of any police on the scene, whether or not they file an accident report.

7. **Make notes on the accident.** Before you leave the scene, do the best you can to draw a diagram of what happened and write down every detail of how the accident occurred. If you have a camera in the car, take pictures of the vehicles' positions and take close-ups of damage to each vehicle.

8. **Do not admit fault.** No matter what you think happened, don't admit fault and never sign anything at the scene.

9. **Call your insurance agent.** Do this as soon as you get home; many companies have a twenty-four-hour number for reporting accidents. The agent will tell you what you should do next.

Before You Talk to a Car Dealer

If you'd like to avoid being taken for a ride (and we don't mean a test drive) the next time you buy a new car, do some homework first. Consumer advocate W. James Bragg describes the smart car buyer as someone who "doesn't rely on the salesman for important information." To buy the car you want at the lowest possible price, follow this checklist, adapted from Bragg's book, *Car Buyer's and Leaser's Negotiating Bible*.

1. **Start with the car you've got.** Find out how much it's actually worth and decide whether to trade it in or sell it yourself. Trading it in means selling it at wholesale; by selling it privately you get the retail price.

2. **Figure out how much money you'll need.** Calculate the monthly payment you can comfortably afford and figure out the down payment based on how much additional cash you can kick in with the proceeds from your current car. The idea is to maximize your down payment and lower your monthly payment.

3. **Shop for money.** Knowing what a loan will cost helps define the upper limit you can afford to pay for that new vehicle. This is a good time to figure what tax and license will cost you for a vehicle in that price range—information the dealer usually won't volunteer until you're committed to the price of the car. Shopping for a loan also helps you evaluate the relative merits of financing deals the car store might offer.

4. **Date dealers, don't marry them.** While you're in this research phase, keep reading up on the models that appeal to you and by all means stop by car stores for test drives. But make it ultraclear that you're there only to shop, not to buy.

5. **Never volunteer information.** You lose your advantage when a salesperson learns how much you're willing to pay, what monthly payment you can afford, and—above all—that you're really excited about a certain car.

6. **Learn the dealer's cost.** Once you've narrowed the field to the two or three models you're considering (including options), find out what each vehicle cost the dealer. The Web site www.carprice.com publishes dealers' invoice prices at no charge. *Consumer Reports* magazine will give you the dealer's invoice cost and the crucial information about current dealer incentives for $12; without knowing about factory rebates and other dealer incentives, you could still end up paying hundreds—or thousands—more than necessary. Keep in mind the dealer's cost, with the incentives and rebates figured in, when you begin negotiating. (A handful of businesses offer more complete assistance to the car buyer, including "coaching" on negotiations. See the "Resources" section on page 293 for more information.)

7. **Memorize these mantras.** Keep these bits of wisdom from Bragg in mind as you prepare to shop for your next car.
   - Eighty percent of a dealer's profits on new-car sales come from 20 percent of his customers.
   - Most dealers make several "slim-profit" deals every month in order to close sales with savvy customers.
   - From the car dealer's perspective, almost any sale is a good sale.
   - It will always be much easier for you to find someone who wants to sell a new car than it will be for a car salesman to find someone who wants to buy one.
   - One reason God gave you feet was to walk away from car salesmen.

✓ Car Insurance: A Rate Reduction Checklist

One of the biggest expenses associated with owning a car is paying auto insurance premiums. Since car insurance is something you can't do without, it's good to know that being a smart consumer can pay off. These tips on reducing auto insurance rates are from the non-profit Independent Insurance Agents of America.

1. **Shop around.** Spending some time on the telephone to research low rates can save you big money. In fact, premiums vary by 50 percent or more among different insurers.

2. **Consider using one company for several policies.** Some insurers give a "fleet discount" for clients who insure more than one car or who use the company for both auto and home insurance policies.

3. **Buy a low-profile car.** Luxury cars cost more to fix and replace, and some "hot" cars have higher theft rates—giving insurers reason to jack up costs.

4. **Stock up on safety features.** Antilock brakes, air bags, and seat belts earn lower rates from nearly every insurance company.

5. **Invest in a security system.** Many companies reward car owners who have alarms, electronic locks, and disabling devises.

6. **Polish your record.** Most insurers give a discount for accident-free driving records. If your record isn't spotless, check to see if your state requires insurers to lower rates for adults who complete defensive driving or accident-prevention classes.

7. **Request higher deductibles.** Increasing the deductible (the amount paid out of your pocket before

the insurance pays) can substantially decrease the premium on the collision and comprehensive portions of your policy.

8. **Buy only what you need.** If you're driving an older car, it may not be worth the money to carry collision and comprehensive coverage (because the book value paid for the car would not be enough for you to replace it). Check with your agent to see what portions of your policy you might want to drop.

9. **Always inquire about discounts.** You never know what a particular company may have to offer.

Conclusion

Now that you have more than one hundred checklists, all neatly provided in book form, you may think you can put away your pencil and never bother writing a list again. Not true! In fact, this book is meant as a starting point for getting organized, asking the right questions—and to getting into the habit of making your own lists.

Your own "to do" lists will likely run the gamut, from groceries to business ideas. But whatever their subject, your lists—like the ones in this book—will serve as a string around your finger, reminding you of what you need to do, and perhaps how or when to do it.

Your lists don't need to be formal (and they certainly don't need to be in a book), but they must be written down somewhere. Keeping a list in your head doesn't count! When a list is rattling around in your memory instead of on paper (or an old candy wrapper or torn envelope), it's unable to perform its chief duty: saving you from your own hectic schedule and forgetfulness.

So pop a notebook into your briefcase and throw a memo pad into your car's glove compartment. You'll welcome the peace of mind that list-making brings.

Resources

Gathering the information for these lists involved a considerable amount of reporting and fact checking. In addition to poring over books, articles and Web sites, I also spoke with many experts who helped me tremendously by sharing their time and expertise. In case you'd also like to tap their talents some time in the future, I'm including some of their names and contact information, along with books and other resources you may find helpful.

PERSONAL SAFETY

National Safety Council, 1121 Spring Lake Drive, Itasca, IL
    60143; 630-775-2307; www.nsc.org
National Fire Protection Association, 1 Batterymarch Park,
    Quincy, MA 02269; 617-770-3000; www.nfpa.org
National Crime Prevention Council, sponsored by Allstate
    Insurance; www.ncpc.org and www.weprevent.org
United States Government Bureau of Justice Assistance;
    www.ojp.usdoj.gov/BJA/

GETTING ORGANIZED

Organizing from the Inside Out. Julie Morgenstern. Henry
    Holt and Company
    www.juliemorgenstern.com;
    E-mail: organize@juliemorgenstern.com
Taming the Paper Tiger. Barbara Hemphill. Kiplinger Books.
Taming the Office Tiger. Barbara Hemphill. Kiplinger Books.

Stocking Up

The Kitchen Survival Guide. Lora Brody. William Morrow &
   Company, Inc.
The Bloomingdale's Home Planner. Bloomingdale's Bridal
   Registry. www.epicurious.com

Home Maintenance

Bob Vila's Toolbox. Bob Vila. William Morrow & Company,
   Inc.
Everyone's Book of Small Hand and Power Tools. George R.
   Drake. Reston Publishing.
*The Complete Guide to Home Maintenance: How to Prevent
   Costly Problems Before They Occur*. Dave Herberle and
   Richard Scutella. Betterway Books.
www.doityourself.com

Housework and Other Emergencies

Household Hints and Tips. Cassandra Kent. DK Publishing.
Hints from Heloise by Heloise. Avon Books.

Flowers and Plants

The 20-Minute Gardener. Tom Christopher and Marty Asher.
   Random House.
Houseplants for Dummies. Larry Hodgson. IDG Books.
The National Gardening Association, www.garden.com
   National Audubon Society, www.audubon.com

Social Life

Entertaining for Dummies. Suzanne Williamson. IDG Books.
Picnic! by Edith Stoval. Storey Publishing.
Weekend!. Edith Stoval and Pamela Wakefield. Storey Pub-
   lishing.
Miss Manners' Guide for The Turn of the Next Millennium.
   Judith Martin. Pharos Books.
Miss Manners' Guide to Excruciatingly Correct Behavior. Judith
   Martin. Galahad Books.
Josh Karin at Geppetto Catering in Washington D.C. 202-
   338-7300.

Correspondence

Emily Post's Etiquette. Peggy Post. Harper Collins.
Also see *Miss Manners* on this topic.

Dealing with Death

It's Your Choice: The Practical Guide to Planning a Funeral. Thomas Nelson. Scott Foresman & Co., an American Association of Retired Persons Book.

The High Cost of Dying—A Guide to Funeral Planning. Gregory Young. Prometheus Books.

McDonough Funeral Home, Belmar, NJ, 732-681-1113

Dying for Business. Marketplace Radio Series. Debra Baer, August 17–September 4, 1998. For audio tapes of the series, visit Marketplace Radio's Web site: www.marketplace.org

Both Direct Casket and Consumer Casket sell caskets and urns directly to consumers at reduced prices. www.directcasket.com www.consumercasket.com

Children (For Those Who Only Borrow Them)

Baby Stuff—A No-nonsense Guide for Every Parent's Lifestyle. Ari and Joanna Lipper. Dell.

Guide to Baby Products. Sandy Jones with Werner Freitag. Consumer Reports Books.

The Babysitter Book: Everything You and Your Babysitter Need to Know Before You Leave the House. Jane Crowley Pardini. NTC/Contemporary Publishing.

Baby Catalogs

Right Start: 800-348-6386
One Step Ahead: 800-274-8440
Land's End Kids: 800-356-4444
L. L. Bean Kids: 800-341-4341
Safety Zone: 800-999-3030
Perfectly Safe: 800-837-KIDS

Moving

Interstate moves are regulated by the Federal Highway Administration of the U.S. Department of Transportation. To see if a mover is registered and insured, call FHWA: 202-358-7106; 202-358-7028; 202-358-7063.

Washington Consumers Checkbook Magazine. Winter/Spring 1998, Vol. 10, No. 4.

Moving, A Complete Checklist and Guide for Relocation. Karen G. Adams. Silvercat Publications.

Barbara and Leon Shoag. This husband and wife team has been selling real estate in the Long Beach, California area since 1981. They have been top award-winners for

the past 12 years and represent about equal numbers of buyers and sellers. They can be reached at 562-427-0669 or by e-mail at bshoag@aol.com.
www.movers.com
www.moverquotes.com
www.moversresource.com
www.realtimes.com
www.springstreet.com

TRAVEL

2002 Tips Even The Best Business Travelers May Not Know. Christopher J. McGinnis. Irwin Professional Publishing.
The Business Travel Survival Guide. Jack Cummings. John Wiley & Sons, Inc.
www.armchair.com
The Business Traveler, www.btonline.com

HEALTH

The Savvy Medical Consumer. Charles B. Inlander. People's Medical Society Handbook.
Health Care Choices for Today's Consumers, Guide to Quality and Cost. Mark Miller, ed. John Wiley & Sons.
Dr. Koop's Self Care Advisor. C. Everett Koop. Time Life Books. www.drkoop.com

THE LAW

Using A Lawyer And What To Do If Things Go Wrong. Kay Osterberg. Random House.
The 90-Second Lawyer. Robert Irwin and David L. Ganz. John Wiley & Sons.
Nolo's Everyday Law Book. Shae Irving, ed. Nolo Press. www.nolo.com.
Everybody's Guide to Small Claims Court. Ralph Warner. Nolo Press.
Collect Your Court Judgements. Gini Graham Scott, Stephen Elias and Lisa Goldoftas. Nolo Press.
Douglas J. Rovens of Rovens, Lamb, Patch and Yocca LLP, Attorneys at Law. 213-895-4150 in Los Angeles. 949-253-0800 in Newport Beach, California.
Waring Fincke, Attorney at Law. E-mail: wrfincke@mail.execpc.com, www.execpc.com/~wrfincke.

YOUR MONEY

Personal Finance

Sue Miller, CPA at Frank & Company, p.c., McLean Virginia 703-821-0702, E-mail: smiller@frankandco.com

Susan Hamilton and Joseph D'Orazio, JD, LLM, CPA, CFP at Rembert, D'Orazio & Fox, financial advisors in Falls Church, Virginia. 703-821-6655.

The Motley Fool, Finance and Folly, www.motleyfool.com Money Management International, www mmi.com, Intelligent Life Corp.'s www.bankrate.com

Choosing a Jeweler

Protea Corporation, Diamond Manufacturers and Wholesalers. Paul Jacobs and Anthony Taitz. 703-536-9822.

Gemological Institute of America. 800-421-7250. www.GIA.com.

Insurance

National Insurance Consumer Helpline. 800-942-4242. A toll-free consumer information telephone service sponsored by insurance industry trade organizations. Licensed agents and trained staff are available to answer questions about a variety of insurance (from life and liability to health, home and auto). Operates Mon–Fri 8:00 AM to 8:00 PM, EST.

Independent Insurance Agents of America, Inc. 800-221-7917. A non-profit industry group offers consumer information and publishes several brochures on a variety of consumer-oriented topics. www.iiaa.org.

Making the Most of Your Money. Jane Bryant Quinn. Simon & Schuster.

PROFESSIONAL LIFE

The Art of Self Promotion Newsletter. Ilise Benun. 800-737-0783. Quarterly publication. $30 for 4 issues. E-mail: ilise@artofselfpromotion.com. www.artofselfpromotion.com

101 Secrets of Highly Effective Speakers. Caryl Rae Krannich. Impact Publications.

Michael Jolkovski, Ph.D. Dr. Jolkovski is a psychologist in the Washington, D.C. area specializing in stage fright. E-mail: MPJolkovski@erols.com

YOUR COMPUTER

"Cheap Computing." Robin Miller, on The Andover News Network. www.andovernews.com.

John Gilroy, "Computer Guy" column can be read bi-monthly in the *Washington Post* and heard on National Public Radio (check with your local public radio station.)

YOUR CAR

How to Keep Your Car Mechanic Honest. Vic and Barbara Goulter. Scarborough House.

What Auto Mechanics Don't Want You to Know. Mark Eskeldson. Technews Publishing.

What Car Dealers Don't Want You to Know. Mark Eskeldson. Technews Publishing.

Car Buyer's and Leaser's Negotiating Bible. W. James Bragg. Random House.

The Savvy Woman's Guide to Cars. Lisa Murr Chapman. Bantam Books.

National Highway Traffic Safety Administration. Hotline: 800-424-9393

www.fightingchance.com

www.carbargains.com

EXCELLENT GENERAL REFERENCE BOOKS

Life's Big Instruction Book. Carol Orsag Madigan and Ann Elwood. Warner Books.

The Home Answer Book. Joanna Wissinger, ed. Stonesong Press.

The Complete Guide to Four Seasons Home Maintenance. Dave Herberle and Richard M. Scutella. Betterway Books.

The Practical Problem Solver. Reader's Digest Books.

Index